CREATING A FINANCIAL PLAN

A How-To-Do-It Manual for Librarians

BETTY J. TUROCK
ANDREA PEDOLSKY

VIKING LIBRARY SYSTEM
204 N. Cascade
PO Box 717
Fergus Falls, MN 56538-0717

HOW-TO-DO-IT MANUALS
FOR LIBRARIES
Number 22

Series Editor: Bill Katz

NEAL-SCHUMAN PUBLISHERS, INC.
New York, London

Published by Neal-Schuman Publishers, Inc.
100 Varick Street
New York, NY 10013

Copyright © 1992 by Betty J. Turock and Andrea Pedolsky

All rights reserved. Reproduction of this book, in whole or in
part, without written permission of the publisher is prohibited.

Printed and bound in the United States of America.

Library of Congress Cataloging-in-Publication Data

Turock, Betty J.
    Creating a financial plan : a how-to-do-it manual for librarians /
Betty J. Turock, Andrea Pedolsky.
        p.   cm. — (How-to-do-it manuals for libraries ; no. 22)
    Includes bibliographical references and index.
    ISBN 1-55570-039-X
    1. Library finance—Handbooks, manuals, etc. 2. Library planning—
Handbooks, manuals, etc. I. Pedolsky, Andrea. II. Title.
III. Series.
Z683.T87 1992
025.1'1—dc20   92-9579
                                                              CIP

FOR FRANK M. TUROCK
THE RUDDER WHO HELPS STAY THE COURSE

IN LOVING MEMORY OF
PETER MARK DELUCA

CONTENTS

ACKNOWLEDGMENTS

Writing a book is a gargantuan task. It is hard to think of anyone doing it without a long list of supporters influencing her work. Grateful acknowledgment is due to the students of financial management at Rutgers University's School of Communication, Information and Library Studies, whose challenging questions helped focus and clarify the material presented here.

To Patricia Glass Schuman, a friend who always sees more in my work than I do, for first convincing me that I had something to say about library finance and enlisting me in her efforts to begin *The Bottom Line: A Financial Magazine for Librarians*.

To the American Library Association's Committee on Planning and Evaluation (COPES) for asking me to present the annual financial planning workshops for the officers of ALA's divisions, and so providing the impetus for me to gather my thoughts into a systematic format. Also, to ALA's Library Administration and Management Association (LAMA) for putting Pat Schuman and me on the road to share what we know with audiences across the country. And to those audiences who gave as much as they got on the nuances of library finance.

But the largest measure of gratitude is saved for my co-author and my family. Without Andrea Pedolsky's unremitting dedication to making certain that this book got to its readers, its ideas could only have been shared in a far more limited way. Finally, my family, and particularly my granddaughter Joy, deserve special thanks. Their encouragement and support make every challenge easier to meet.

BJT

When Pat Schuman and Jack Neal first suggested that I team up with Betty Turock to write this book I thought: But I'm an editor, not a writer. Nonetheless I agreed, motivated by the challenge—and the opportunity to work with Betty once again. A year of weekends spent together writing (and well cared-for by Frank Turock) passed. The manuscript grew—and along with it my admiration for Betty. She has great knowledge of and insight into libraries—and infused this book with both. It has been an enjoyable collaboration.

Like Betty, I received much support and love from friends and family. Mom, Dad, Sheldon, Stephen, Myles, Eva, Ada, and Angela—thank you.

And Jack and Pat, thanks for the challenge and for believing I could meet it.

AP

INTRODUCTION

We are living in a time when financial accountability through expert financial planning is crucial to the viability of libraries. Like all organizations, libraries are economic entities. From the smallest library open only a few days a week to a major research library, all have funds that have to be managed, accounted for, and disbursed. In addition, all libraries operate within a larger environment. The librarians who manage them must compete for finite, limited resources and make the most from what they get.

Whether you are a director of a library or a manager of a department within a library, you undoubtedly are responsible for executing some—if not all—of the library's financial affairs, which means you are a financial manager, even if your job title doesn't specifically state it. That responsibility makes it imperative for you to advocate and employ financial planning in your institution.

Your ability to analyze and plan is a powerful skill. But the end result of financial planning is more than just adding numbers to a preexisting plan. Financial planning will help you control your library's destiny. That's why we've written this book. It is designed to present you with an understandable yet challenging introduction to the sequence of thought- and action-taking steps that will leave you better prepared to face the fiscal future.

Part One begins with a discussion of the fundamentals. In Chapter 1 you will learn how to begin thinking about financial planning; the importance of a financial plan to the well-being of your library; the tasks and responsibilities of the library manager; the politics of financial planning, including who the key players are; how the library manager controls the process; and how to deal with the inevitable resistance that inaugurating financial planning will bring.

Part Two covers the data-gathering process necessary to produce the documents that comprise your financial plan. In Chapter 2 you'll learn about financial data that are important to collect on an ongoing basis. You'll be introduced to the design and function of the balance sheet and the types of ratios of fiscal health that can be computed from it. Annually, when a new balance sheet is created, you will discover how comparing the new with the old helps measure the progress you've made in improving your library's financial outlook.

In Chapter 3 you'll focus on the specifics of your library by completing a situation analysis. You'll dissect the impact on your library of such external factors as the economic, legal, social, technological, organizational, and political conditions prevailing nationally, as well as regionally and locally. In addition, you'll examine the library's internal conditions, such as work distribution and productivity.

You'll gain evidence of how effectively resources are being used in Chapter 4, by completing a market analysis of your library's programs: What is the comparative level of support among your services? Who are your current customers? What potential customers are as yet unreached? What new services might reach them?

The financial planning process is a vigorous program of looking back to see how things worked in the past, examining the present to decide whether things are working as they should be, and setting priorities for the future. Thus, the work you complete in Part Two forms the basis for the three-year plan you begin in Part Three. Here you'll see that the situation and market analyses aren't ends in themselves. They play an equally important role in helping the library manager know how much funding the library will need on an annual basis over the life of the financial plan. In Chapter 5 you will begin inventing solutions for the problems identified in Part Two by setting financial goals and objectives—without which the library would stagnate.

Rather than taking the crystal ball approach, in Chapter 6 you will learn how to forecast expenditures the library will incur over three years to offer responsive services, while at the same time seizing new service opportunities. This chapter also discusses how to link budgetary forecasts with annual budgets. In addition to laying out the differences among budget formats—line-item, program, performance, and zero-base—you will learn how to develop a budget for your library that builds on the priorities arising from the situation and market analyses and articulated in the goals and objectives.

Income is the lifeline of the library; it needs ongoing and sufficient resources to keep it robust. Strategies available for increasing your funding are described in Chapter 7. That's where we emphasize the design of a development program that targets new sources of income, encourages diversification, and sets the framework for using money to make money through investments. No matter how worthy your goals, objectives, and strategies are, they are only words until infused with money to put them into action and disseminate the plan to decision makers.

In Part Four you'll check the course of your financial plan.

Chapter 8 presents ways to evaluate its success and then update it. You'll learn the methods you can employ to determine whether you are making the right financial moves, and if your plan needs modifying. Finally, Chapter 9 describes the function of the Executive Summary and emphasizes the importance of communicating the results of the plan to library stakeholders and funding decision makers. The financial planning model designed in this book focuses on the public library, but it is equally adaptable to academic, special, and school library settings.

There are currently several library management books available that guide planning. Others guide evaluation efforts. Still a third group addresses costing and finance. But none bring all three functions together in a comprehensive or systematic way. When you have completed this book, you will have produced a set of documents that connects your library's priorities and service performance with its allocation of resources. That, we believe, is the unique contribution of *Creating a Financial Plan*.

PART ONE

THE FUNDAMENTALS

1 FINANCIAL PLANNING AS STRATEGIC PLANNING

The overarching goal of any library is to continue to respond to community needs regardless of economic fluctuations. It is not difficult to experience success at this when resources are on the rise. It becomes far more difficult when they are declining. Creating and using a financial plan can help maintain or improve your library's services in any economic climate.

PURPOSES OF FINANCIAL PLANNING

The primary purpose of the financial plan is to document your library's fiscal strategies and focus its efforts for a three-year period, which is a workable planning schedule in these times of rapid technological change, escalating costs, and increased competition.

Think of your financial plan as an action agenda. It is the platform from which you determine and measure your library's need for funds; raise the necessary funds and allocate them; make certain the funds are used properly; evaluate the impact of new investments and programs on your library's operations; ensure accurate financial reporting; analyze financial results; and set future projections to ensure the efficient and effective use of resources. The financial plan will also help you conduct library operations in a fiscally responsible way. It will allow you to make mistakes on paper rather than in practice.

Among the reasons for preparing a financial plan, the most important is to cultivate a solid and diversified funding base for your library. Developing a financial plan will show potential funders how you are preparing to meet the library's future needs. The financial planning model for libraries borrows heavily on the underpinnings of the corporate business plan in this regard.

As a retrospective evaluation tool against which you can assess performance over time, the financial plan shows whether the library has been able to stick to its budget and still meet its goals and objectives. The success with which that is accomplished gives a measure of the success of the plan itself. Evaluating the plan

By creating a financial plan, the library manager will be better able to

—define and quantify the library's overall service goals and objectives in monetary terms
—assess progress in meeting financial goals and objectives
—establish indicators that will identify significant deviations in the library's use of its assets
—provide direction in safeguarding the library's assets
—allocate technical, human, organizational, and financial resources to support service priorities
—attract potential funders

3

THE RAILROAD
The Pennsylvania Railroad was once considered one of the best-managed corporations in the world. When hard times from labor troubles, obsolete equipment, and increased competition came to the rail industry, it struggled to survive but eventually went out of business. What's telling about its plight is that, when asked to describe its mission, the PRR answered, ''Railroading.'' Its surviving competitors, on the other hand, responded with a broader perspective: ''Transportation.''

periodically permits you to see where the library strayed from what was set out and determine whether straying was helpful or harmful.

THE BASICS

A successful financial plan will answer two fundamental operational questions. The first concerns accountability: How can we make *effective* use of our resources to respond to our community's needs? The second question concerns productivity: How can we make *efficient* use of our resources outside and within the library environment?

The financial plan is comprised of eight basic segments. This book is organized to parallel them:

An analysis of the library's financial status: What is the library's current financial condition? (Chapter 2)

A situation analysis: What economic, legal, political, social, technological, and organizational factors are impacting on the library and shaping its financial future? (Chapter 3)

A market analysis: Who comprises the library's current and potential customer base? Are the library's current and potential programs, services, and products responsive to their needs? What is the library's competition? (Chapter 4)

Assumptions about the future: What are the library's financial goals and objectives, which will help demarcate the path the library will take for a healthy financial future? (Chapter 5)

Three-year outlook: Budgetary forecasts for three years that will feed into the formulation of annual operating budgets and bring financial challenges into clearer focus. (Chapter 6)

Funding strategies: What alternative sources of funding will pay for the library's growth and development? (Chapter 7)

Evaluation: An evaluation of the financial plan so that you know whether you are on the right track. (Chapter 8)

Executive Summary: A concise version of your financial plan to communicate your library's case for support to fiscal decision makers. (Chapter 9)

TASKS OF THE LIBRARY MANAGER

The library manager's responsibilities are neatly dictated by the process of financial planning. It is no simple task, but it will place you squarely within the intricate mechanisms of the operational and programmatic functions of your library.

Financial planning will introduce change into your library. Change inherently brings resistance, since we all have conflicting demands for order, structure, dependability, and predictability on one hand and excitement, stimulation, and variety on the other. It is through this complexity that the library manager will have to maneuver warily if financial planning is to be successful.

Until their roles are clarified, staff may feel vulnerable, concerned that they lack the knowledge and skills needed to participate in financial planning. In fact, they may lack knowledge because of limited opportunities for mastering financial skills in library education programs. Their perception that financial planning is an extremely difficult, time-consuming process with uncertain benefits can be countered by attention to five preliminary stages that will get them ready for participation:

1. Create a planning environment
2. Form the financial planning team
3. Determine team training needs
4. Time and sequence team activities
5. Implement the process

CREATE A PLANNING ENVIRONMENT

Of course, introducing financial planning will be considerably more welcomed if your library has already developed an environment in which change is not unusual—in which change is accepted as improving on the library's successful past.

If this is a first-time experience in planning, a few actions will help set a positive scene: Emphasize the benefits that will accrue from having a well-drawn financial plan. Recruit participants from all staff levels, not just top management, so that all feel they have a stake in the process and so that you can gain their commitment to making it successful. Watch for reluctant planners. You'll want to pay special attention to them through all phases of the process so they don't derail progress midstream. Before you start, make clear what the process is going to entail, stressing that staff involvement is key to the success of the planning endeavor. Of course, top management must be committed to financial planning. Make that commitment obvious from the start.

FORM THE FINANCIAL PLANNING TEAM

Your financial plan will not be worth the time and money it takes to complete it if it doesn't provide the information necessary to impact policy-making and future programmatic decisions. Its success is largely dependent on your ability to seek and obtain input, advice, and participation for the team from external as well as internal stakeholders—those who have a share or an interest in the library and its future.

The internal stakeholders—staff members—will provide representatives to the financial planning team from all service units in the library. In addition to top management, they should include other librarians and clerical staff so that their valuable nonmanagerial perspective is available. This group conducts the data collection, analysis, and interpretation.

Some staff will show more interest in financial planning than others. Enlist them immediately as advocates for the process, encouraging others to join in its implementation. Encourage their full involvement. This will strengthen their participation not only in this change but in the many other changes that will surely confront the library over time.

The external stakeholders—members of the community—are chosen as the result of their leadership positions and through a nominating process conducted by the internal team. When nominating candidates, consider the following criteria. The team will need people who are:

- knowledgeable about the community and the needs of its diverse population
- recognized leaders
- accessible
- nonusers as well as users of the library's programs
- successful fundraisers

Some external team members are easily identified. For the public library, they would be drawn from the board, community financial decision makers, state library representatives, and leaders of special interest and action groups. For the corporate library, the stakeholders would include managers whose portfolios contain the library or information center, as well as representatives from the corporation's major departments. For the academic library, members of the administration (particularly those holding financial positions), faculty, and students are likely candidates. For the school media center, principals, teachers, students, and parents could comprise the team.

As you make your way through the financial planning process, be sure to share results with the external stakeholders for feedback. This will not only help them become an active part of the process, but it will strengthen their support for the plan as a whole. Of course, some external team members may offer resistance to financial planning. For example, you may find that a trustee or member of the parent organization's management team doesn't understand its importance, and therefore sees no need to provide resources to create a financial plan. This could be a hard sell, especially if your library has "managed fine without one." Just as with staff, tout the benefits of financial planning. As the opportunity for greater fiscal control unfolds, you will have the strong likelihood of turning an opponent into a champion.

The major contribution the external team makes to the process is in helping the internal team recognize political realities early in the game. It serves as a source of information in the data collection phase and acts as a response group to check the authenticity of the internal team's data analysis and interpretation. It helps ensure that the financial plan correctly represents life in the community your library serves. When they are involved in the process, external stakeholders are indispensable in developing interpretations that have meaning for financial decision makers.

DETERMINE TEAM TRAINING NEEDS

Staff expertise will have a strong influence on the success of your financial plan. The tasks required can't be so complicated that the staff is unable to handle them. If your staff doesn't have sufficient expertise, you may find it cost- and time-effective to hire a consultant. Professional financial planners or librarians with financial planning experience can facilitate the process, but the activities still should be performed by the team, which is ultimately responsible for the plan's implementation.

It is doubtful that staff will possess all of the skills needed for financial planning, but a training program that encompasses the necessary elements can build the skills they will need while at the same time building a fiscal focus. An orientation session for all staff is a good lead-in to the process. There you can ask participants to complete an anonymous questionnaire listing the skills needed for creating the plan. Respondents can then check off areas in which they feel weak. To stimulate participation, include the roles available in financial planning and ask respondents which they would like to assume. Based on the results of the skills survey,

STAFF TRAINING NEEDS

Each chapter in this book presents a major component in financial planning. You can prepare a checklist using the chapter headings for distribution to staff to discover their training needs. Then organize the skills essential for participation under these headings. Set up group training sessions that review the entire process and highlight those areas in which most staff indicate they need assistance. The sources at the end of the book supply the background and additional reading for staff members interested in pursuing any of the topics in greater depth.

you can make sure the staff's educational needs are taken care of in the preliminary phases of the effort.

TIME AND SEQUENCE TEAM ACTIVITIES

It is essential to maintain control of the sequence of activities in financial planning as well as their timing and duration. Creating a graphic timeline will help you keep to your schedule. Figure 1-1 is an example organized by major activities, the approximate time allotted to them, and their expected completion dates. You can also prepare a more detailed timeline that outlines activities by precise beginning and end dates, the staff assigned to their completion, and the time allocated, as illustrated in Figure 1-2.

The duration of financial planning will depend on the point at which you enter the process. You may have already completed the market analysis, for example, which would reduce the total time required.

The time projections depicted in the models are subject to modification to meet the unique conditions of your library. Decide the level of effort you will dedicate to financial planning. Higher levels will cost more in resources—staff, time, and money. The Public Library Association's *Planning and Role Setting* establishes first-rate guidelines to assist you in determining the level that's right for you.[1] Library size is clearly a factor in determining the effort required. Other key determinants are:

> *Participants:* Involving more people increases the amount of effort required.
> *Environment:* Libraries serving communities with rapid growth, change, or complex and diverse populations need higher levels of effort.
> *Structure:* More complex library organizations require higher levels of effort, since the process must flow through more formal channels.

The level of effort given over to financial planning may also vary from phase to phase. The duration shown on the timeline models is based on a high level of effort spread over a 12-month period.

The "planning to plan" process, including orientation and training, will set the scene for the entire endeavor, so this is not the place to cut corners. Data gathered to analyze the library's current financial status, situation, and market can be initiated concurrently. Since a determination of financial status will result from a new look at historical data, with little or no need for original compilations, it will take less time than either the situation or market analyses. Setting fiscal assumptions, goals, objectives,

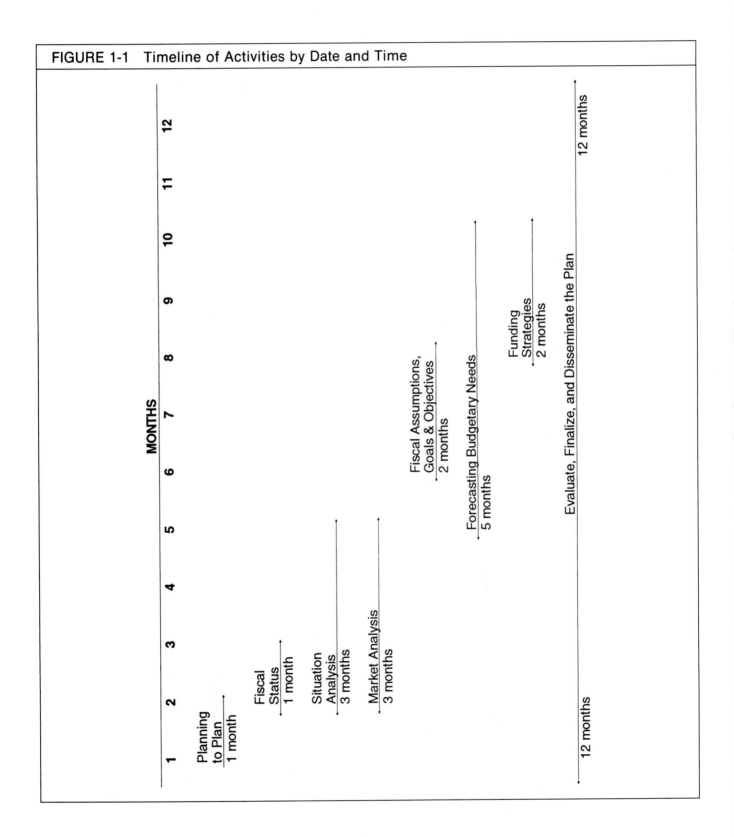

FIGURE 1-1   Timeline of Activities by Date and Time

FIGURE 1-2   Timeline of Activities by Date, Time and Staff

Financial Planning Activities	Dates Begin	Dates End	Staff Assignments	Time Allocation in days By Staff Member	Total
1. Plan to plan	Month 1	Month 2			
2. Analyze current fiscal status	Month 2	Month 3			
3. Conduct situation analysis	Month 2	Month 5			
4. Conduct market analysis	Month 2	Month 5			
5. Make assumptions and set financial goals and objectives	Month 6	Month 8			
6. Forecast budgetary needs	Month 5	Month 10			
7. Invent strategies	Month 8	Month 10			
8. Evaluate, finalize, and disseminate the plan	Month 1	Month 12			

Meet The New Age Library

To illustrate the work of the financial planning team and the situations they might encounter as they initiate the financial planning process, we have built a series of scenarios around the New Age Library and its financial planning team. The approaches they develop to collect, analyze, and interpret the data they compile for their financial plan are meant to act as a catalyst to your thinking and open new options to help you meet your library's financial challenges.

The New Age Library

MISSION STATEMENT
The fundamental purpose of the New Age Library is to provide our community with the right information, in the right form, at the right time, while ensuring the most cost-effective use of resources. The library acts as a conduit to and from other external information sources and services.

and strategies are group activities, which increases their duration. Budget preparation is a 12-month proposition. The five months designated on the timeline are what is required to prepare your forecast.

Writing the final plan is a task best given over to one team member, but it will require review by the financial planning team, the library's staff, and policy-making bodies. Evaluation is ongoing throughout the entire planning period. In each phase of the process, evidence will be collected that will lead to future improvements in the way in which financial planning is conducted, as well as in the financial plan itself.

IMPLEMENT THE PROCESS
It is impossible to design a financial planning model that can be implemented in all libraries without modification, but there are some principles that apply across the board. The financial planning team must be consistent in collecting data, reporting findings, formulating strategies, and recordkeeping. Formats must be agreed upon and deadlines set. Decide early in the process who will do what. Communicating with the entire library staff on the progress of the plan is crucial to its ultimate acceptance and utility. Let them know their ideas are valued and that they are part of the plan's feedback loop by:

- paying particular attention to any activity that may intrude on the normal functioning of the library, for example, the initiation of a productivity study
- letting the staff review the results of each of the plan's segments as they unfold and asking them for their input before the final version is put together
- circulating the milestones in financial planning, explaining important aspects so that everyone knows what is taking place and what is at stake

FOUNDATIONS OF THE FINANCIAL PLAN

As you begin to focus on the strategic purview of the financial plan, you must first consider the driving force behind it: the mission statement, which establishes your library's identity. It is the written and agreed-upon guiding principles that set out the

The New Age Library

GOALS AND OBJECTIVES

For the next three years, the New Age Library has set two related top-priority goals to be reached through several objectives.

Goal 1: The Library will serve a larger number of groups now underserved.

Objective 1: Complete a market analysis of the community within four months to identify who is underserved.

Objective 2: Increase the number of active library users by at least 10 percent in the next two years.

Goal 2: In cooperation with local agencies, the Library will initiate services that enhance the economic viability of the community.

Objective 1: Contact agencies that work with the major underserved groups (adult as well as youth, identified as at-risk) and develop collaborative plans within the current year to mobilize services for them.

Objective 2: Capture 20 percent more users from at-risk groups over the next three years.

library's purpose so that decisions can be made with unity and effectiveness. Broadly construed so that it remains valid through times of change, the mission statement answers three basic questions:

- Who are we?
- Why are we here?
- What is our business?

The library's mission is a clear statement from which you can derive its goals and objectives and direct its services and priorities. It provides the overall context for the financial plan and serves as the starting place to which you can return whenever you are trying to maintain consistency in setting your financial strategies.

The library's mission statement gets its roots from the mission statement of its parent organization: the local government, if a public library; the university, if an academic library; the corporation, if a special library. As a result, both the library's mission statement and that of its parent institution are operative in financial planning, and both are points of reference for library managers in their day-to-day work and in moments of crisis.

Do you know your parent organization's mission statement? Take the time now to reacquaint yourself with it and write it out in full on Worksheet 1-1. Then, on Worksheet 1-2, place your library's mission statement.

While your library's mission statement points to the direction in which you want to move, goals and objectives are the guideposts to its tomorrows. They set *in detail* what you want the library to attain in the future. More flexible than the mission statement, they are subject to regular alteration to respond more immediately to changes in the library's environment. Goals supply a holistic vision of what the library hopes to accomplish in the long term and act as end points toward which activity is directed, helping the library move forward.

Objectives are concrete, measurable, and/or verifiable expressions of the library's desired short-term ends. They are precise, attainable, and focused on the results to be produced in a fixed period of time. Like the mission statement, the library's goals and objectives are set in motion by your parent organization's goals and objectives.

In Chapter 5 you will develop your library's financial goals and objectives. Since they evolve from the general goals and objectives of your parent organization as well as your library, take the time now to enter these general goals and objectives on Worksheets 1-3 and 1-4.

WORKSHEET 1-1   The Parent Organization's Mission Statement

WORKSHEET 1-2   The Library's Mission Statement

WORKSHEET 1-3 The Parent Organization's Goals and Objectives

Goal #1:

Goal #2:

Objective:

Objective:

Objective:

Objective:

Objective:

Objective:

Goal #3:

Goal #4:

Objective:

Objective:

Objective:

Objective:

Objective:

Objective:

WORKSHEET 1-4   The Library's Goals and Objectives

Goal #1:   *Goal #2:*

Objective: Objective:

Objective: Objective:

Objective: Objective:

Goal #3:   *Goal #4:*

Objective: Objective:

Objective: Objective:

Objective: Objective:

The New Age Library

VALUES

As it set out on its financial planning course, the New Age Library reaffirmed the following values:

- The library should provide the maximum possible service to its community

- The services and programs of the library should be responsive to community needs

- The library's most valuable resources are its community members and its staff

- Financial support allocated to the library reflects a commitment on the part of the community to the work of the library through the development of its services and programs

- The library as a whole exists in an environment of mutual programmatic and financial interdependence with its parent organization and with other libraries in the state and across the nation

MATCHING RESOURCES TO PRIORITIES

Financial planning focuses your attention on strategic ends to make certain that your programs have continuing value to the community you serve. Making decisions without considering their impact on future programs and operations could lead your library in undesired directions. Peter Drucker was right on the mark when he observed that the financial plan tells your money where to go so that you don't have to spend your time finding out where it went!

The most frequent complaint about financial planning is that it allows numbers to replace values, so that the bottom line drives programs and services. But the object of financial planning is to ensure that values, not finances, drive priorities. Unplanned, short-term expediency is a far greater threat to library values. Financial planning is neither value-free nor value-neutral. One of its important benefits comes from the articulation of values through the association of goals, objectives, and services with the money needed to realize them.

Before we begin collecting data for the plan itself, set out your library's values on Worksheet 1-5.

LONG-TERM OUTLOOK

Financial planning is concerned with the long-term management of library resources. It translates the library's overall goals and objectives into dollars and cents, then allocates resources to reflect the priorities established. Financial planning also helps you attain control of your library's operations and offset fiscal uncertainties. With a financial plan in hand, you'll have the ammunition to fight the conventional wisdom that the only way to expand an existing service or initiate a new one is to increase revenue or decrease support for other services.

So let's get started by moving on to Part Two, where you'll collect a variety of data from which you will build your library's financial plan.

WORKSHEET 1-5 The Library's Values

Reaffirm your library's values here. Choose those you think will have the greatest impact on the financial planning process.

ENDNOTE

1. Charles R. McClure, Amy Owen, Douglas Zweizig, Mary Jo Lynch, and Nancy A. VanHouse, *Planning and Role Setting for Public Libraries* (Chicago: American Library Association, 1987), 10, 16, 29, 49, 58, 69, 76.

PART TWO

DATA GATHERING

2 CURRENT FINANCIAL STATUS

The first task before the members of your financial planning team is to determine the fiscal health of your library. You can accomplish this through a series of analyses and by producing a number of comparisons based on the library's balance sheet. You will be looking back to discover the trajectory of your library's fiscal affairs.

WHAT ACCOUNTING SYSTEM DOES YOUR LIBRARY USE?

How your library records its financial transactions will affect the accuracy with which you can document your financial status at any time. Two basic accounting systems exist for this purpose: cash and accrual. The main difference between them is *when* a transaction is recorded. *Cash accounting* recognizes and records transactions only when cash is received or disbursed. For example, income is recorded when an overdue fine is paid, a donation is made, or a check is received for profits from duplicating machine usage. As bills are paid and cash is received, an entry is recorded for each transaction. In other words, a transaction is recognized only when it involves an inflow or outflow of cash. What the library owes and what it is owed are not taken into consideration.

Accrual accounting provides a more complete picture of an organization by matching income earned with expenses incurred. It records income and expenses at the time transactions occur. For example, let's say that your library has ordered and received a new $1,600 video camera to continue developing its local history collection. Using the accrual system—although you haven't paid the bill and don't plan to pay it for 30 days—you have to record the expense of $1,600 under accounts payable in your financial records because you have incurred the obligation. Using cash accounting, the transaction is not recorded until you write the check for payment.

Here's another example. Perhaps your library sometimes receives advance payments for services expected, like the total allocation awarded through a grant before all or even part of the services due under the contract are performed. Cash accounting would record the total income received when the check arrives. Accrual accounting would record amounts only when services are rendered.

Cash accounting results can vary significantly from fiscal reality. The accrual method is more accurate and less susceptible to manipulation and distortion. Account balances can be influenced on a cash basis by controlling the timing of check disbursements. For example, if you order and receive $5,000 worth of books but don't pay the bill, your account will not reflect the $5,000 obligation under the cash system; it will reflect it under the accrual system.

MAKING SOUND FINANCIAL DECISIONS

Sound financial decisions tilt the scale toward accrual accounting. More and more auditors are recommending accrual accounting to libraries as part of their audit reports to ensure that financial statements are as accurate as possible.

Even those libraries not required by law to do so might want to invest in having their financial statements audited annually to determine their reliability. In the audit, an examination and a check of the library's financial statements is made by an independent Certified Public Accountant (CPA) to verify and sanction the correctness of the library's financial reports and reporting mechanisms. When the auditors complete their task, they issue an opinion indicating how well the library has conformed with Generally Accepted Accounting Principles (GAAP), the rigorous standards established by the American Institute of Certified Public Accountants.

If the statements have no problems, you will be given what is called a clean opinion. If the auditors find problems, you will receive a qualified opinion and be expected to address the problems cited. The qualified opinion will stand until the auditors return, reexamine the financial statements, and render a clean opinion. The auditors will also write a management letter which provides further analysis of their views of library management's budgetary controls and reporting.

Audits add credibility to the library's financial operations and point out new directions that can lead to future improvements, not only in recordkeeping, but also in financial planning. As library managers grapple with greater and greater public demand to demonstrate fiduciary responsibility by wisely caring for assets held in trust, the audit is one means of making the quality of their financial stewardship clearer.

THE BALANCE SHEET

The key to the audited financial statement is the balance sheet. It provides a snapshot of the fiscal health of the library on a particular day in its life. It is used to compare where your library is now with where it was at the same time last year. It also offers a comparison of the status of the library's assets—what it owns— and liabilities—what it owes—at the end of an accounting period.

Figure 2-1 shows the New Age Library's balance sheet at the start of the current fiscal year, after it received the first of two regular infusions of cash from its parent organization. It has two main sections, one covering assets, the other covering liabilities.

Assets and liabilities can be presented in one of two ways. As in Figure 2-1, assets can be listed first, at the top half of the balance sheet, with liabilities following at the bottom. Or, they can be presented side by side, with assets on the left and liabilities on the right. The fund balance—or net worth—appears at the bottom of the sheet or on the right. It is the surplus of assets over liabilities. Total assets always equal the combined total of liabilities and fund balance. That's why this is called a balance sheet.

ASSETS

Assets are positioned on the balance sheet in the order of their liquidity—according to the speed with which they can be converted into cash. There are two classes of assets: current and fixed. Cash is the most liquid current asset. Other examples are short-term investments, like Treasury bills and Certificates of Deposit; inventories, like supplies; and receivables, or any money owed to the library that can be collected.

Fixed assets are generally acquisitions that cost more than $1,000 and are planned for long-term use. Examples include land, buildings, equipment, and furniture. When expressed on the balance sheet, their value takes depreciation into consideration.

LIABILITIES

Liabilities also are categorized as current or fixed. Current liabilities are those due for payment within the fiscal year. Fixed liabilities represent longer-term debt. In Figure 2-1, you can see accounts payable, accrued expenses, and the current portion of the mortgage listed as current liabilities. There is one long-term liability representing the total owed on a mortgage, minus the current portion of the mortgage figure.

FIGURE 2-1 New Age Library Balance Sheet

	CURRENT FUNDS		BUILDING EQUIPMENT FUND	ENDOWMENT FUND	TOTAL
	Unrestricted	**Restricted**			
ASSETS					
Current Assets:					
Cash	$594,842	$ 425	$ 415		$ 595,682
Short-term securities	2,753			$ 8,000	10,753
Fines and fees receivable	884				884
Grants receivable		30,000			30,000
Supplies	225		420		645
Total Current Assets	$598,704	$ 30,425	$ 835	$ 8,000	$ 637,964
Investments			12,200	8,962	21,162
Land, buildings, and equipment			1,860,000		1,860,000
Total Assets	$598,704	$ 30,425	$1,873,035	$16,962	$2,519,126
LIABILITIES AND FUND BALANCES					
Current Liabilities:					
Accounts payable	160,000	12,000			172,000
Accrued expenses	82,900				82,900
Current mortgage payment			120,600		120,600
Total Current Liabilities	242,900	12,000	120,600		375,500
Total Mortgage Payable			675,000		675,000
Total Liabilities	$242,900	$12,000	$795,600		$1,050,500
Fund balances:					
Unrestricted	355,804				355,804
Restricted:					
Literacy		10,425			10,425
Programming		8,000			8,000
Purchase of fixed assets			67,435		67,435
Invested in fixed assets			1,010,000		1,010,000
Endowment funds				16,962	16,962
Total Fund Balance	$355,804	$18,425	$1,077,435	$16,962	$1,468,626
Total Liabilities and Fund Balances	$598,704	$30,425	$1,873,035		$2,519,126

FUND BALANCE

The bottom line in the nonprofit sector is referred to as the fund balance. In the for-profit sector it is called net worth. The balance sheet of the nonprofit organization is actually divided into separate accounts, or funds, containing more categories of data than will be found in a for-profit organization. Even though the nonprofit balance sheet is more complex, the rules for constructing it are common to both environments.

The fund balance has two functions. First, it expresses the residual between assets and liabilities. Second, it summarizes the year's difference between the inflows of resources and incurred expenses. The fund balance as residual is what we all respond to in a very concrete way. If liabilities are larger than assets, the balance is in the negative and described as "in the red" or "in the hole." When expenses are higher than resource inflows, a decrease occurs in the fund balance.

Then there is the good news, when assets are greater than liabilities. Now, the balance is positive, and the organization is described as being "in the black." When resource inflows are larger than expenses, the fund balance experiences an increase.

BALANCE SHEET EQUATIONS

Assets = Liabilities + Fund Balance

Fund Balance = Assets − Liabilities

Liabilities = Assets − Fund Balance

DEPRECIATION

Depreciation plays an important part in constructing your balance sheet. It represents the decline in useful value of a fixed asset due to wear and tear from use, the passage of time, and obsolescence. It is actually a bookkeeping entry which allows you to allocate the cost of a piece of property or equipment over its useful life. A portion of the cost is charged to the financials each year, even though there is no cash outlay after the first year.

When the New Age Library purchased a $50,000 computer system compatible with the regional multitype network of which it is a member, it opted for a five-year depreciation schedule. This means that only the first of the five years was counted as a depreciation expense—in this case, $10,000. For the next four years, $10,000 was charged to the financial statements as a noncash expense. And so, depreciation was a cost for one year, and a source of funds for four years.

Three methods are available to depreciate a fixed asset: the straight-line, the accelerated, and the double-declining balance. The straight-line method is commonly used in libraries. It allows you to take equal amounts of depreciation expense each year, as the New Age Library did with its $50,000 computer system. Using the accelerated method, more depreciation expense is taken in earlier years. With the double-declining balance, the rate is calculated at twice the straight-line method.

WORKSHEET 2-1   Balance Sheet

	CURRENT FUNDS		BUILDING EQUIPMENT FUND	ENDOWMENT FUND	TOTAL
	Unrestricted	**Restricted**			
ASSETS					
Current Assets:					
Cash					
Short-term securities					
Fines and fees receivable					
Grants receivable					
Supplies					
Total Current Assets					
Investments					
Land, buildings, and equipment					
Total Assets					
LIABILITIES AND FUND BALANCES					
Current Liabilities:					
Accounts payable					
Accrued expenses					
Current mortgage payment					
Total Current Liabilities					
Total Mortgage Payable					
Total Liabilities					
Fund balances:					
Unrestricted					
Restricted:					
Literacy					
Programming					
Purchase of fixed assets					
Invested in fixed assets					
Endowment funds					
Total Fund Balance					
Total Liabilities and Fund Balances					

For an asset that is likely to diminish in usefulness more rapidly at the front end of a purchase, either the accelerated or double-declining method is the best choice. For instance, a library vehicle would be treated by one of these methods because automobiles lose their value rapidly once they leave the showroom. The straight-line is most effective for items whose obsolescence occurs over the usual period of depreciation—five years. A library's photocopying machines, for example, are best treated by this method. Now, using Worksheet 2-1, create your library's balance sheet.

RATIO ANALYSIS AND THE BALANCE SHEET

In itself, the balance sheet is a collection of figures that supplies you with a good deal of information. But when a series of balance sheets are regularly interrelated, they begin to tell you not only where your library stands financially, but also whether its current course is a healthy one. Usually, a sharp decline in assets is cause for concern; a sharp decline in liabilities is cause for celebration.

You can also derive value from your balance sheet by using its data to compute ratios. Two of the most useful are the current ratio and the acid-test ratio.

CURRENT RATIO

The current ratio is a measure of liquidity. It indicates the ability of an organization to pay its bills. Measures of liquidity answer questions like: "Do we have sufficient cash, plus assets that can be turned into cash, to ensure that we can pay the debts that are expected to fall due during this accounting period?"

The current ratio is computed from the balance sheet by dividing current assets by current liabilities. Using the New Age Library's balance sheet, the current ratio would be computed as follows:

$$\text{Current Ratio} = \frac{\text{Current Assets}}{\text{Current Liabilities}} \text{ or } \frac{\$637,964}{\$375,500} = \$1.70$$

In this case, the ratio is $1.70 to $1. This means that for every dollar the New Age Library owes, it has $1.70. If the ratio were less than $1, it would show that the library couldn't pay its bills. A one-to-one ratio would mean that the library could just make ends meet. The ratio in this example says that the New Age Library has some maneuvering room.

In the for-profit sector, a ratio of two to one is considered optimum—the organization would be described as healthy. Most nonprofit organizations can accept lower ratios than those acceptable in for-profit organizations because their long-term financial base is considered more stable.

THE ACID-TEST RATIO

Sometimes called the quick ratio, this is more stringent than the current ratio because it is calculated on only the most liquid current assets, like cash, short-term securities, fines receivable, and grants receivable. It is more meaningfully applied to the for-profit sector, where receivables and inventories are higher. The acid-test is computed here using the New Age Library's balance sheet in Figure 2-1.

$$\text{Acid-Test Ratio} = \frac{\text{Cash} + \text{Short-term Securities} + \text{Receivables}}{\text{Current Liabilities}} \text{ or } \frac{\$673,319}{\$375,500} = \$1.69$$

In this case, the ratio is $1.69 to $1.

There is little difference between the ratios in the preceding examples because the New Age Library's inventory of supplies and its receivables are low—a usual case in the nonprofit sector. When ratios are too low, new financial strategies may be introduced, like paying off a debt or divesting the library of some of its assets.

Now let's look at your library's balance sheets for the last three fiscal years to discover trends. On Worksheet 2-2, fill in the assets, liabilities, and fund balance, or net worth. The ideal situation is an increase in assets and fund balance, accompanied by a decrease in liabilities.

On Worksheet 2-3, calculate your current ratio as well as your acid-test ratio using the figures for year three. Go back to your balance sheet to retrieve the dollar figures for cash, fines receivable, grants receivable, and short-term securities. What do these calculations and comparisons indicate about your library's financial status?

WORKSHEET 2-2   Trends in the Balance Sheet

Fill in the assets, liabilities, and fund balance from your balance sheets over the last three years:

	Assets	Liabilities	Fund Balance
Current Fiscal Year			
Fiscal Year 1 (1 year ago)			
Fiscal Year 2 (2 years ago)			

Describe the trends you see in:

Assets:

Liabilities:

Fund Balance:

WORKSHEET 2-3   Current Ratio and Acid Test Ratio

Current Ratio   = $\dfrac{\text{Current Assets}}{\text{Current Liabilities}}$ or $\dfrac{\$\underline{\hspace{3cm}}}{\$\underline{\hspace{3cm}}}$ = $ \underline{\hspace{2cm}}

Acid Test   = $\dfrac{\text{Cash + Short-term Securities + Receivables + Supplies}}{\text{Current Liabilities}}$ or $\dfrac{\$\underline{\hspace{3cm}}}{\$\underline{\hspace{3cm}}}$ = $ \underline{\hspace{2cm}}
Ratio

INDICATORS OF FISCAL HEALTH

Analyzing trends over a period of time will add to the picture of your library's fiscal health. The important indicators for this analysis are: total income, total expenditures, the library's sources of income, and expenditures by specific categories.

Worksheets 2-4 and 2-5 ask you to identify trends—growth or decline—in your library's income and expenditures. You can calculate the trends in these two categories by subtracting the past year's figure from the present year's and dividing by the past year:

$$\text{Trends} = \frac{\text{Present Year} - \text{Past Year}}{\text{Past Year}}$$

For each of the worksheets, fill in the last three fiscal years, excluding the current year, of your library's total income and total expenditures. An effective way to illustrate the trends is to plot the numbers on a graph. You can use Worksheets 2-6 and 2-7 to track your library's dollars and trends.

WORKSHEET 2-4 Trends in Library Income

What trends can you identify in the aggregate fiscal growth/decline of your library's income over the past three years?

	Total Library Income	Trend (% +/−)
Current Fiscal Year		NA*
Fiscal Year 1 (1 year ago)		
Fiscal Year 2 (2 years ago)		

To complete this worksheet, fill in the last three years of your library's total income. To determine the growth or decline, use the following formula:

$$\frac{\text{Present year} - \text{Past year}}{\text{Past year}} = \text{Trend}$$

WORKSHEET 2-5 Trends in Library Expenditures

What trends can you identify in the aggregate fiscal growth/decline of your library's expenditures over the past three years?

	Total Library Expenditures	Trend (% +/−)
Current Fiscal Year		NA*
Fiscal Year 1 (1 year ago)		
Fiscal Year 2 (2 years ago)		

To complete this worksheet, fill in the last three years of your library's total expenditures.
To determine the growth or decline, use the following formula:

$$\frac{\text{Present year} - \text{Past year}}{\text{Past year}} = \text{Trend}$$

WORKSHEET 2-6 Tracking the Dollars

To complete this worksheet, place relevant dollar amounts in incremental sums along the vertical axis. Then, using dollars calculated on Worksheets 2-4 and 2-5, plot the three years of dollars and connect the dots to form a visual representation.

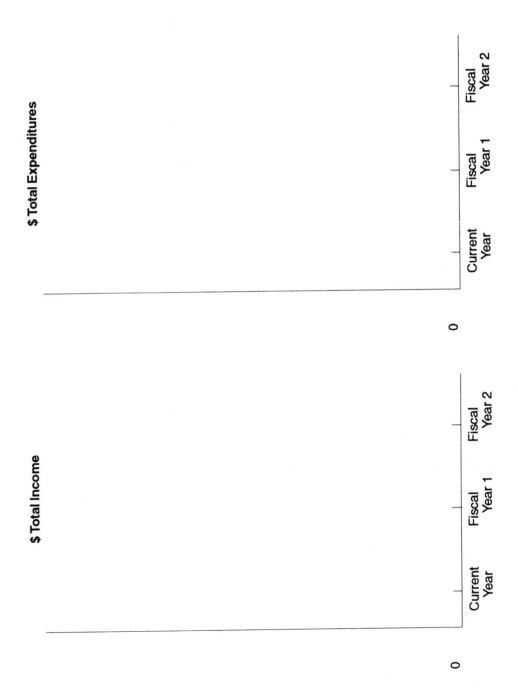

$ Total Income

$ Total Expenditures

WORKSHEET 2-7 Tracking the Trends

To complete this worksheet, place relevant percentages in incremental stages along the vertical axis. Then, using the percentages calculated on Worksheets 2-4 and 2-5, plot the three years of trends and connect the dots to form a visual representation.

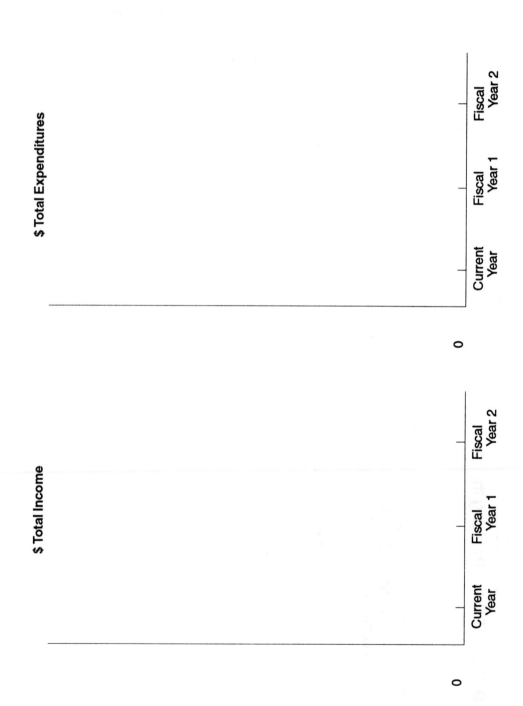

$ Total Income

$ Total Expenditures

Next, on Worksheet 2-8, you can identify library expenditures by filling in specific budgetary categories for the last three fiscal years, excluding the current year. We have provided you with a beginning list of broad categories for which your library probably makes expenditures. Of all the worksheets in this chapter, Worksheet 2-8 will give you the most detailed information about where your library's money is going because you will discover what percentage of total expenditures is used by each specific expenditure category.

Finally, you'll want to capture your library's current sources of income. Worksheet 2-9 includes a list of possible source categories. Add and delete what you must so that the final categories depict your library's current situation. Compiling such a list will help you determine how diverse your funding base is. It may show that you need to diversify further—particularly in bad economic times, when it's important to have a mix of sources. Looking at your income over a three-year period will help bring to mind which sources you stopped receiving funding from, and which might prove to be viable once again.

WHAT IS YOUR LIBRARY'S CURRENT FINANCIAL STATUS?

Knowing where your library's dollars come from and go to is crucial to controlling expenses, containing costs, and stabilizing cash flow. With these data in hand, you have taken the first step in understanding your library's future financial challenges. When the New Age Library's financial planning team reviewed the information they had gathered, they discovered that over the past three years the library's expenses had grown faster than its income.

You may find your library in similar circumstances. How you interpret the data you've collected will be based on the special characteristics and conditions of your library. Now you can begin to zero in on trends that demand attention if your library is to continue to thrive.

WORKSHEET 2-8 Expenditures by Specific Budgetary Category

What are the library's expenditures by specific category* over the last three years?

	Current Year		Fiscal Year 1		Fiscal Year 2	
	$	%*	$	%	$	%
Personnel						
Materials						
Books						
Periodicals						
Databases						
Documents						
Supplies						
Office						
Computer						
Communication						
Postage						
Telephone						
Datalines						
Conferences						
Staff Development						
Other						
Total						

To compute percentage of total, divide each expenditure category by the total amount of expenditure.

*Adapt list of expenditure categories to best reflect your library.

WORKSHEET 2-9 Sources of Income

What were the library's sources of income over the last three years? To compute percentage of total, divide each source of income by total amount of income from Worksheet 2-4.

	Current Year		Fiscal Year 1		Fiscal Year 2	
	$	%*	$	%	$	%
Taxation						
Endowment						
Grants						
Federal						
State						
Corporate						
Private Foundation						
Community Foundation						
Other						
Gifts						
Investments						
Bond program						
Contract-for-service						
to libraries						
Annual Campaign						
Direct Mail						
Other						
Tributes and memorials						
Membership programs						
Fees						
Photocopying						
Reserves						
Fees for service						
Other						
Fines						
Overdues						
Other						
Sales						
Buttons						
Bookstore						
Tee shirt						
Other						
Special Events						
Used book sale						
Author reception						
Library anniversary						
Raffle and auction						
"Thon"						
Other						

3 THE SITUATION ANALYSIS

All organizations are affected by conditions outside and within their immediate environments, and libraries are no exception. In order to plan for the future—and deal intelligently with day-to-day activities—library managers must be aware of both the global and local conditions under which they are operating. The situation analysis will help you identify external conditions and their impact on your library's ability to deliver its programs and services effectively. It will also help you redeploy resources by identifying those internal conditions that affect economies.

EXTERNAL CONDITIONS

The situation analysis focuses on six critical external forces: economic indicators, the legal environment, social conditions, technological outlook, organizational restructuring, and political factors.

ECONOMIC INDICATORS

Economic conditions that prevail globally affect all of us locally. Key indicators bear watching because they give early-warning signs of the general health of the economy. It's like getting advice from several financial advisors, then checking one against the other to see if there is a consensus. The indicators point to whether we are on an upward or downward economic trend. Ironically, it is during economic downturns that library use increases—at the same time that the usual minimal funding declines sharply.

Library managers frequently track the path of the Gross National Product (GNP), which is the total value of new goods and services produced in the economy. If growth in the GNP wanes, libraries' fortunes usually follow. If it is robust, libraries can expect to fare well. To make the best possible financial decisions it is useful to follow other economic indicators as well, including:

Fluctuation in the interest rate on three-month Treasury bills: This is the current rate investors are demanding in return for their money. When interest rates rise, corporate profits tend to go down, which portends less money in circulation for local services.

Settlement of major labor contracts: The level of the settlement can be an indicator of an inflationary trend.

Strength of the U.S. dollar: Drops in the value of the dollar lead to rises in the costs of foreign goods, another sign of inflation on the horizon.

Payroll and unemployment figures: As the number of employees on company payrolls rises, so does consumer spending and the stock market—good signs for the times.

Standard & Poor's 500 stock average and The Dow Jones Industrial Average: Upswings in these indexes indicate a rise in corporate profits, also a good economic omen.

When the New Age Library completed its economic analysis, the findings were unmistakably grim. The national economic downturn had impacted extremely negatively on its community. There were many empty shops on Main Street, and the local unemployment rate was outpacing the national level.

THE LEGAL ENVIRONMENT

No library function or program is free from the effects of the law and its regulations. Affirmative Action and Equal Opportunity Employment Programs are the results of federal laws that continue to move libraries toward the multicultural work force of the twenty-first century.

We also have witnessed the effects of the enactment of the Tax Reform Act of 1986. Not only did it do away with the business lunch as a personal tax deduction, but it also reduced the deduction allowable for donations to nonprofit organizations. As a result, volunteer fundraisers lost their deduction for wining and dining potential donors and libraries lost one of the key incentives available to them for enticing donor gifts.

SOCIAL CONDITIONS

As an embodiment of our democracy, libraries traditionally have had an open-door policy to any one wanting to make use of their services. In fact, outreach to nonuser populations is a standard technique public libraries use to expand their clientele. The services and programs libraries offer at least in part reflect the social conditions in their communities. Expanding services to meet the needs of latchkey children and the unemployed are two examples.

When libraries are hard-hit financially, the services ordinarily

TRACKING FEDERAL ALLOCATIONS

The two important federal funding sources are the Library Services and Construction Act (LSCA) for public libraries and Title II of the Higher Education Act (HEA) for academic libraries. Both laws have been reauthorized every five years, but seldom without extensive revisions or shifts in entitlements within their purview.

Depending on the politics of each presidential administration, the response of Congress to the executive budgetary recommendation, and the general economic climate of the country, more or less money goes to support LSCA and HEA. When libraries find less money forthcoming from the federal government, it is a bellwether for state and local funding as well. That's why it is so important to track executive recommendations and congressional actions and to contact your Washington representatives and senators as soon as they begin to discuss the possibility of decreases for libraries.

available are often cut back or totally eliminated. The impact on local residents can be heavy, for example, when a library cuts back its hours or closes branches.

TECHNOLOGICAL OUTLOOK

Although managers were once the chief agents of change in organizations, they no longer are; technology has taken their place. The rate of technological innovation is so rapid that organizations constantly question how frequently they have to expand or enhance their systems.

Libraries are not strangers to the dilemma of wanting—indeed, having—to be technologically up-to-date in order to provide the best possible service and to run the best possible library operations. Being up-to-date means dealing with the high cost of technology.

Take, for instance, the online public catalog (OPAC) and CD-ROM, both of which have had significant impact on libraries' ability to provide access to information and materials. Libraries without these technologies have to decide at what point they can no longer afford *not* to have them. Libraries already using them have to decide when to upgrade in order to continue offering optimum service.

Technology is also a powerful agent of change in our personal lives. For example, over 80 percent of U.S. households own a VCR. In response to this, libraries have increased their collections of videocassettes. This, in turn, has raised the issue of fees for library services. It is likely that every library with a circulating collection of videocassettes asks itself the fee-or-free question. Since new technology always is accompanied by new media formats, libraries must repeatedly question whether and how to add them to their collections.

ORGANIZATIONAL RESTRUCTURING

In times of rapid change, libraries may find themselves restructuring to improve their ability to deliver services. They may, for instance, establish a new neighborhood information center, move a branch or satellite, or join a library network. At one time the typical library was bound by local jurisdiction (home rule). But over the last decade, the greatest amount of structural change has been effected by libraries joining multitype networks.

POLITICAL FACTORS

Politics impact heavily on a library's bottom line. In every election, libraries face the possibility of losing a supporter—or gaining one. On a local level, changes in the administration can alter to whom

POWER BASE CHANGES WITH REGIONALIZATION

In the early 1980s, the New Jersey legislature allocated the money to support the State Library's regionalization using a multitype library network model. The new infrastructure changed how resources were shared and how grants were awarded. It also redistributed the state's power base. Libraries now have to bid on contracts and compete for money. Many accustomed to receiving a big piece of the financial pie no longer do. As a result of these changes, some libraries grew into powerhouses overnight, while other powerhouses died.

library managers report and their access to financial decision makers. Consider, for instance, the effect of sending to Congress a representative who is an ardent supporter of libraries rather than one who thinks the tax revenues allocated for libraries are too high.

The community where the New Age Library is located is an example. In their recent election, a pro-library councilperson won by a landslide. Now the library has an important advocate in city hall.

UNDER WHAT EXTERNAL CONDITIONS IS YOUR LIBRARY OPERATING?

Understanding your current external environment and how it is affecting the library will help you make assumptions about the future in which the library will operate. By taking a look at these six external factors: economic, legal, social, technological, organizational, and political, you can begin to ferret out what changes must be incorporated into the way your library does business to meet the challenges ahead. Take the time now to fill out Worksheets 3-1 through 3-6.

On Worksheet 3-1 you will describe the economic climate the library faces: Is this a time of growth or economic downturn? Will you see any changes in the future? How will the economy influence the library? By completing Worksheet 3-2 you'll outline any new legislation and regulations governing the library and their impact. Worksheet 3-3 asks you to think about the social conditions your constituents are experiencing.

On Worksheet 3-4 you will consider the available technology and analyze what you believe the library must acquire to maintain or improve services. On Worksheet 3-5 you'll review recent restructuring and determine what it has meant to your library. Finally, on Worksheet 3-6 you will sketch out the political climate your library operates in and how it affects your funding. You will refer to these worksheets again in Part Three.

INTERNAL CONDITIONS

The focus of the second half of the situation analysis is determining your library's efficiency. Of course, it is also crucial to review the condition of your physical plant, union contract provisions, work force stability and adequacy, and their effects on operating costs. Cost analyses are equally important. They let you

WORKSHEET 3-1   Economic Indicators

What national economic conditions are impacting on your local community? Is it experiencing economic growth, downturn, inflation, recession, etc.? Describe how the economic conditions are affecting the library's ability to finance programs, products, and services.

WORKSHEET 3-2   Legal Environment

Investigate changing laws and regulations. Describe how they are impacting on your library's financial ability to support programs, products, and services.

WORKSHEET 3-3 Social Conditions

What social conditions are impacting on your local community? How are they affecting your library's programs, products, and services?

WORKSHEET 3-4 Technological Outlook

What technology is available to assist in the delivery of programs, products, and services? What must the library acquire to maintain its programs, products, and services? How will its acquisition affect your operations financially and programatically?

WORKSHEET 3-5   Organizational Restructuring

What changes are occurring in the way your library's service environment is structured? Describe how new library configuations are impacting on your library's funding and ability to deliver programs, products, and services.

WORKSHEET 3-6   Political Factors

Examine the political environment in which your library operates—on national, state, and local levels. How is it influencing funding and how might it change in the next election?

WORKSHEET 3-7   Library Efficiency

How efficiently do you think your library performs? Write down particular areas where you would like to see improvement.

---

determine the real costs of services, track costs over time, and measure the feasibility of alternative service modes. A comprehensive costs analysis model that is adaptable to all types of libraries is available in Philip Rosenberg's *Cost Finding* (ALA, 1985).

Measuring efficiency is emphasized here because libraries tend to give it scant professional attention, even though it has great potential for revealing how we can redistribute our funds to increase service while holding the line on costs—or maintain service when funding erodes.

Begin by completing Worksheet 3-7. This is an impressionistic form on which you can describe your perceptions about your library's efficiency and the areas in which it might improve.

MEASURING EFFICIENCY
Two types of analyses will provide you with information that highlights ways to improve operating efficiency: work distribution and productivity studies. Work distribution follows staff through the steps they perform in doing their jobs. It looks at the sequential order of activities leading to the completion of tasks in order to pinpoint which areas of the work load are inefficiently distributed.

Productivity studies provide another measure of efficiency by indicating the percentage of staff time devoted directly to performing the tasks of a job, or output per hour.

There are a number of key developmental steps required. The first is to create a list of tasks involved in the area under investigation, then define and describe each task. Figure 3-1 is a partial list of cataloging activity definitions written by the New Age Library's work distribution study participants. The financial planning team pinpointed the cataloging department as the first of several service units to conduct a work distribution study.

The second key step is to create a work distribution time log chart—Figure 3-2 shows one of the New Age Library's. All staff members in the study complete a new chart each day of the week, compiling time and units processed in each activity, then adding them at the end of the week. At the end of the study period— usually no less than two weeks—the data are aggregated for all staff. Total time is translated from minutes into hours. Then the output per hour is computed by dividing the total time by the total units processed.

Next, an estimated unit cost can be determined—in this case, the funds spent to catalog one item. It is calculated by adding up for the period studied the cost of: salaries and fringe benefits, supplies, technology and other equipment, administration, and utilities; then, dividing that sum by total units processed. Rosenberg's *Cost Finding* outlines a more exact way to compute unit costs using the data gathered in the work distribution study.[1]

You can compare the charts both individually and against each other. This will help you pinpoint areas of unbalanced work loads and develop recommendations for improved work assignments. The New Age Library's study, for instance, led the financial planning team to conclude they must attend to:

Misdirected effort: The library found that a good deal of time was spent reclassifying materials coming over OCLC to fit their modified classification schedule.

Inefficient use of skills: Librarians were opening and sorting boxes of books.

Unrelated tasks: One librarian was verifying bibliographic records through local holdings, then switching over to entering data into OCLC. When further verification was needed, someone else continued it through the use of standard tools.

FIGURE 3-1   New Age Library's Cataloging Activity Definitions

1. *Receive, Sort, Distribute Incoming Items:* Items are received from acquisitions. They are sorted and distributed by type to the appropriate person: new singles, rushes and best sellers, foreign language, paperbacks, juvenile, and audiovisual.
2. *Searching OCLC:* Locating catalog copy for each item without CIP, each item not found earlier, and each item rechecked.
3. *Other Bibliographic Verification:* Searching authority and shelf-list for call numbers and/or main entries for sets and fiction.
4. *Original Cataloging:* Descriptive cataloging, subject analysis, classification, analytics, and authority work are performed where no LC copy or adequate cataloging data are available. A cataloger prepares a work form or work sheet to be used for catalog record production or for input into OCLC.
5. *Production/Reproduction/Printing of Catalog Records:* OCLC production, local production, and mechanicals are noted here. The downtime on OCLC should be included when it interferes with the process.
6. *Revision of Catalog Records:* Locally reproduced records are proofed and OCLC records are sorted.
7. *Alphabetizing Catalog Records:* Main catalog records to be withdrawn or corrected and media are alphabetized.
8. *Preparing/Revising Pockets, Book Cards, and Stickers:* Note here revising masters, revising run-off pockets, matching pockets with set cards for acquisition, preparing pockets.
9. *Special Handling:* Include here large print, musical scores, bestsellers, and other rushes.
10. *Catalog Maintenance:* Corrections, including weeding, are entered here.
11. *Error Reports:* Enter here time spent, number made, and time required to write up.
12. *Supervision, Administration, Training, Meetings, Staff Development, Peer Consultation, Telephone:* Any time spent in supervising nonstandard work, including personnel within the department; administrative duties such as correspondence, staff review, reports, budgeting, statistics, supplies, payroll, mail; training new personnel for duties; conferring with associates; professional reading, staff or professional meetings; or telephone answering should be entered here. DO NOT INCLUDE LUNCH BREAKS OR SICK OR VACATION LEAVE. Do not include time for which you are not paid.
13. *Unassigned Time:* Coffee breaks or lunch time for which you are paid that is spent on other than job-related duties.
14. *Data Collection for This Study:* Enter time spent in filling out this form or reviewing procedures or definitions for this study in this category.

FIGURE 3-2   New Age Library Time Log Chart

Department _____

Name _____

Date(s) _____

Enter below the time spent and volume processed in each activity listed. Work distribution charts should be completed by each employee for each day over a period of two weeks. Entries should be made as a task is completed, filling out TOTAL boxes at the end of the day. At the end of each week aggregate the total number of units and minutes. Round off times to the nearest 5 minutes (e.g., 48 minutes should be entered as 50). Don't include lunch periods. Indicate UNITS PROCESSED by inserting the number of items completed. Note FORMAT as: books, cassettes, etc.

WORK DISTRIBUTION TIME LOG CHART

Activity*	Format	Time (in minutes)	Units Processed
1. Receive, sort, distribute incoming items		Total:	Total:
2. Search OCLC		Total:	Total:
3. Other bibliographic verification		Total:	Total:
4. Original cataloging		Total:	Total:
5. Production/ Reproduction/ Printing		Total:	Total:
6. Grand total			
Output per hour** =			

Note: * This is a selected list of cataloging activities from definitions
       ** Output per hour = Total time/Total units processed

Overspecialization: Only one librarian cataloged AV materials. When she was absent from work, no one else was prepared to do the job.

Too many people on one task: Everyone was inputting New Age Library information into the OCLC database, while other tasks were not well covered.

Repetition: Clerks who opened boxes upon their receipt in the shipping room were checking invoices against the shipment. This task was then repeated in the cataloging room.

Outmoded equipment: Because there were not enough personal computers for the cataloging team, one member had to do original cataloging on an electric typewriter. If another staff member had to work on the same data, it had to be processed a second time.

Inefficient facility layout: In order to catalog fiction books, staff had to cross the floor three times when arranging the shelving close to catalogers' desks could have eliminated this excess movement.

If you decide to do a time log, these eight problem areas will be important to analyze. Use the time log on Worksheet 3-8 to get started.

MEASURING PRODUCTIVITY

We've been hearing more and more about productivity measurement, a technique for increasing efficiency. No longer an indicator in the blue-collar workplace alone, productivity measurement is now used in all types of work situations. Its benefit is clear: you will find ways to streamline operations.

The Work Distribution Time Log stores the data needed to measure productivity. The Staff Utilization Report, found in Worksheet 3-9, shows the route you will follow to arrive at your library's productivity figures. Figure 3-3 shows you the calculations of the New Age Library's financial planning team for one activity: searching OCLC:

Column A: The activity (search OCLC) is taken from the completed time log.

Column B: The unit of measurement in this case is each item searched.

WORKSHEET 3-8   Time Log Chart

Department _____

Name _____

Date(s) _____

Enter below the time spent and volume processed in each activity listed. Work distribution charts should be completed by each employee for each day over a period of two weeks. Entries should be made as a task is completed, filling out TOTAL boxes at the end of the day. At the end of each week aggregate the total number of units and minutes. Round off times to the nearest 5 minutes (e.g., 48 minutes should be entered as 50). Don't include lunch periods. Indicate UNITS PROCESSED by inserting the number of items completed. Note FORMAT as: books, films, filmstrips, records, cassettes, periodicals, etc.

WORK DISTRIBUTION TIME LOG CHART

Activity	Format	Time (in minutes)	Units Processed
		Total:	Total:
		Total:	Total:
		Total:	Total:
		Total:	Total:
Grand Total			
		Total:	Total:

WORKSHEET 3-9   Staff Utilization Report

A. ACTIVITY	B. UNIT BEING MEASURED	C. # UNITS PROCESSED	D. ALLOTTED HOURS	E. MEASURED HOURS	E/D = F F. STAFF PRODUCTIVITY

FIGURE 3-3 Staff Utilization Report: Cataloging Department

A. Activity	B. Unit Being Measured	C. # Units Processed	D. Allotted Hours	E. Measured Hours	F. E/D = F Staff Productivity
Search OCLC	Each item searched	4,000	200	150	.75

Column C: Houses the expected number of units processed. At the New Age Library, an average of 100 searches was performed by each of the four staff members per day over the two-week study period of ten working days (at 5 hours a day), for a total of 4,000 searches: $100 \times 4 = 400 \times 10$ days $= 4,000$ units processed.

Column D: The allotted time for the task is 200 hours (5 hours a day $\times$ 10 days $\times$ 4 staff $= 200$ hours.

Column E: Total measured hours is taken from the time log study. Since it measures the activity in minutes, you divide by 60 to get total hours. The New Age Library's time log added up to 9,000 minutes. 9,000/60 minutes $= 150$ hours.

Column F: Staff productivity is calculated by dividing the number of measured hours in Column E (150) by the total allotted hours in Column D (200). The New Age Library found a productivity ratio of .75.

If, when you complete your Staff Utilization Report, your productivity measure ranges between 75 and 85 percent, this shows a solid performance. Anything below 75 percent tends to indicate excess staff on the activity measured, staff that can be reassigned where they are needed more. A measure of 100 percent or more would cast doubt on the reliability of your data.

EFFICIENCY AND QUALITY

Up to this point we have stressed the quantitative aspects of efficiency. But efficiency must be infused with a qualitative component as well. Regardless of how productive a library is, unless the service is acceptable to the people for whom it is intended, it is worthless. Twice a year the New Age Library asks its users to express their assessment of the quality of library service. You'll find the survey they used in Figure 3-4.

To create a measure of quality, you should periodically survey your customers to monitor their experience with the library's performance. For measures of customer satisfaction to be valid, survey data should be collected from 300 to 400 users, criteria set for the level of satisfaction the library wants to meet, and at least

---

FIGURE 3-4   User Survey

NEW AGE LIBRARY USER SURVEY

Date: _____

* *
Please complete this questionnaire today and return it to a staff member on your way out of the library. Please circle the letter to all answers that describe your visit to the library. YOUR ANSWERS WILL HELP US IMPROVE.
* *

1. I came to the library today to:
   A. Find particular books or other items by looking for titles.
   B. Find something by a particular author.
   C. Find general information about a particular subject.
   D. Find particular facts to answer specific questions.
   E. Look around for something of interest.
   F. Bring my children.
   G. I came for another reason: _____

   _____

   _____

   _____

   _____

2. If you were looking for something in particular, did you find it? Please list up to 4 subjects, facts, titles, or authors and check whether or not you found them.

I looked for:	Total	I found it	I didn't find it
Subject			
Facts			
Title			
Author			
Total			

3. My reason for coming to the library today was:
   A. Job related
   B. School related
   C. To pursue personal interests and/or spend leisure time
   D. No response

FIGURE 3-4 (*Continued*)

4. On today's visit to the library:
   A. I checked out books.
   B. I checked out an item other than a book.
   C. I used books in the library.
   D. I used newspapers and magazines in the library.
   E. I used items other than books, newspapers, and magazines in the library.
   F. I did not use any library materials because I could not find the material that I came for.
   G. I used other library facilities or services: _____

   _____

   _____

   _____

   _____

5. How did you get to the library, that is, what means of transportation did you use to get here?
   A. Motor vehicle, drove myself
   B. Motor vehicle, rode with someone
   C. Public transportation
   D. Bicycle
   E. Walked

6. On today's visit, parking was:
   A. A problem
   B. Not a problem
   C. N/A

7. On today's visit, finding a place to sit was:
   A. A problem
   B. Not a problem
   C. N/A

8. During today's visit, library staff:
   A. Were readily available and helpful
   B. Were readily available but not helpful
   C. Were not readily available

9. On today's visit, the part of the library's collection of most interest to me was: (Please name subject or category, for example: HOME REPAIR, FICTION, etc.)

   I found the collection in this area to be:
   A. Excellent
   B. Adequate for my needs
   C. Too limited
   D. Not current enough

FIGURE 3-4 (*Continued*)

10. On today's visit my use of the catalog was:
    A. Essential for finding what I was looking for
    B. Very helpful
    C. Somewhat helpful
    D. Not helpful

11. I have had a library card at this library:
    A. For more than five years
    B. For between one and five years
    C. For less than a year
    D. Have no card of my own

12. Which of the following changes would increase your satisfaction with the library (CIRCLE ALL LETTERS THAT APPLY)
    A. No changes necessary
    B. Library open on Sunday
    C. Increased evening hours
    D. More attractive buildings
    E. More books for adults
    F. More books for teens
    G. More books for children
    H. More records
    I. Videocassettes
    J. Better information services
    K. Better staff services
    L. More staff
    M. More library programs for children
    N. More library programs for teens
    O. More library programs for adults
    P. Services for the homebound
    Q. Other (please specify): _____
    _____
    _____
    _____
    _____
    _____
    _____
    _____
    _____

FIGURE 3-4 (*Continued*)

13. I visit this library:
    A. At least once a week
    B. At least once a month
    C. Less than once a month
    D. This is my first visit
    E. No response

14. I am age:
    A. 0–4
    B. 5–12
    C. 13–19
    D. 20–34
    E. 35–55
    F. 56–64
    G. 65 +

15. I am:
    A. Student
    B. Employed
    C. Unemployed
    D. Houseperson
    E. Retired
    F. No response

16. My last or current school level is:
    A. Elementary—
       1–4
       5–8
    B. High School—
       1–2
       3–4
    C. College—
       1–2
       3–4
    D. Graduate
       1–2
       3 +

17. My current occupation is:
    A. Professional
    B. Technical & managerial
    C. Sales & clerical
    D. Skilled

18. My current income is:
    A. Less than $7,500
    B. $7,500–14,999
    C. $15,000–19,999
    D. $20,000–24,999
    E. $25,000–29,999
    F. $30,000–34,999
    G. $35,000–39,999
    H. $40,000–44,999
    I. $45,000–49,999
    J. $50,000–54,999
    K. $55,000–59,999
    L. $60,000–64,999
    M. $65,000–69,999
    N. $70,000–74,999
    O. $75,000–99,999
    P. $100,000 +

THANK YOU FOR COMPLETING THIS QUESTIONNAIRE

average scores computed for each of the questions asked to determine how well the library meets the criteria.

Efficiency, quality, and customer satisfaction are more than buzzwords. In both the profit and nonprofit sectors, the focus is on bringing the three together in day-to-day operations. Although responding to users has traditionally held the attention of library managers, most have not considered how combining quantitative and qualitative analyses of efficiency can impact on customer satisfaction. But in an age of fiscal scarcity, we can no longer disregard the relationship among the three and the library's bottom line.

ENDNOTE

1. Philip Rosenberg, *Cost Finding for Public Libraries* (Chicago: American Library Association, 1985), 16–19.

4 THE MARKET ANALYSIS

The financial plan that you devise will arise in large measure from an assessment of your library's effectiveness in serving its customers. By performing a market analysis, you will be prepared to answer two key questions in that assessment:

1. Who comprises the population the library is chartered to serve?
2. How well does the library meet the needs of that population?

Market analysis is a means of defining your library's customers precisely, identifying their needs, and determining whether their numbers are growing, declining, or staying constant. It measures the appeal your library's services have for various target groups and suggest barriers—real or perceived—that deter people from seeking out and using them. It looks for evidence of how interested your target audiences are in the services you currently provide or might project for the future. Market analysis makes the financial plan more externally directed—addressing the needs of the library's customers, identifying opportunities to satisfy them, and making more effective use of available funding.

The market analysis will help the financial planning team understand the uniqueness of the marketplace so that your library can improve its responsiveness. Its two major segments are the Community Profile and the Library Profile.

The Community Profile involves collecting and analyzing data about the makeup of your service area, channels of distribution the library uses to deliver its services and programs, and the library's competitors. The Library Profile measures performance using a broad range of indicators, both qualitative and quantitative. As a result, you will derive information on the level of resources supporting the library's programs and services vis-à-vis the size and type of your audiences. It also includes a review of the library's promotional activities to determine their adequacy.

THE BUILDING BLOCKS OF MARKET ANALYSIS

The Community Profile and the Library Profile are the building blocks of the market analysis. They supply data that may either support the continued allocation of resources as they are currently

How Responsive is Your Library?

Since one of the cornerstones of a financial plan is subjective analysis, have each member of your financial planning team indicate with a check mark how responsive they think your library is to its customers.

Then, compare and discuss your answers.

OUR LIBRARY IS:

_____ responsive

_____ highly responsive

_____ fully responsive

The market analysis will help you become more responsive by compiling a body of data that profiles your library and the community, comparing the two, checking the fit between them, and highlighting areas that need improvement. With these data in hand, you will probably have a different feel for your library. At the end of the chapter, you will consider your answer once again.

distributed or act as a directive for their redeployment. But the market analysis doesn't just examine the library's current situation; it also helps you plan for the future.

With the data collected in the Community Profile, you can analyze the potential for attracting new customers, for developing new channels of delivery, and for facing the competition. From the data collected in the Library Profile, you will be able to consider what services might be improved or added to attract new users and what types of promotional activities you will use to reach new target audiences. Putting the two together will help you improve the library's responsiveness quotient.

THE COMMUNITY PROFILE

It is axiomatic that, if a library is to provide responsive services to its customers, it must know its community. So the objects of the Community Profile are to gather a complete and accurate picture of the population your library is chartered to serve and to determine what group or groups the library currently is not serving at all (or is not serving as fully as possible). It may confirm what you already know, or it could signal changes about which you are not aware. This profile asks that you dig into the makeup of your community. The data you gather also will help you sharpen the focus of the Library Profile.

You can think of the Community Profile as the development of information for target marketing. The key step is market segmentation, which is the act of dividing constituencies into distinct and meaningful groups that might merit separate services. For the Community Profile, libraries generally have classified target markets by geography and demography.

FACTORS IN THE SERVICE SETTING

Look at your community in terms of its setting, which influences library users' need for and response to your programs and services. There are seven basic areas for you to consider: history and topography, cultural and social organizations, educational systems, communications networks, transportation systems, political characteristics, and community services. In the following section, you will find suggested questions and sources of information for finding answers to them.

HISTORY AND TOPOGRAPHY

What affect does the history and development of the community have on the library?

What affect do physical and natural geographical features have on community patterns of library use?

Can and will the residents come to the library or must you go to them?

Sources: Maps; local government reports; local, regional, and state planning agencies; Chamber of Commerce; walking and driving through the community; local history collections.

CULTURAL AND SOCIAL ORGANIZATIONS

What public and private recreational services and facilities are available? Where are they located?

What and where are the major cultural institutions (e.g., museums, galleries, theaters)? What services do they offer?

What cultures and interests are represented by these organizations?

Do the organizations and their members have special information needs?

Are organizations available for various age groups?

Are there active volunteer groups?

Sources: Newsletters, brochures, and annual reports of religious, social, and cultural organizations; directories; community bulletin boards; exhibits and fairs.

EDUCATIONAL SYSTEMS

What are the number, level, and location of channels for formal education?

What is the quality of local school media centers?

How do children and young adults get to school?

What channels for informal education are offered? Who participates in them?

Sources: Elementary and secondary school district offices; adult schools; colleges and universities; cultural and social organizations.

COMMUNICATIONS NETWORKS

What formal and informal communications networks are available?

What kinds of services do they provide?

Are there special interest networks? What are they?
What is the range and depth of coverage of local, regional, and national events, issues, and decisions as presented by the media?

Sources: Radio, television, and cable station managers; newspaper and magazine publishers and editors; support groups; neighborhood groups; community leaders; crisis services.

TRANSPORTATION SYSTEMS
Is the community compact or spread out?
Are there barriers that impede transportation?
How do traffic patterns influence residents' behavior?
Is a public transportation system available?
How accessible is the library to the community?

Sources: Transportation authorities; automobile clubs; police departments; schedules from public transportation offices.

POLITICAL CHARACTERISTICS
How active are residents in the electoral process?
Where is the decision-making power in the community?
What is the relationship of the library to various governmental units?
What are the trends in political strength? Political structures?
What is the position of the library in the political structure?

Sources: Governmental offices; political organizations; political figures; government officials; directories; League of Women Voters.

COMMUNITY SERVICES
What kinds of services does the community support (e.g., hospitals, nursing homes, special schools, detention homes, jails, prisons, training centers, rehabilitation centers, homes sponsored by religious groups, halfway houses, shelters for the homeless)?
How large is each service and where is it located?
Are there advocacy groups for the special populations served by these agencies?

Sources: Health and welfare agencies; service organizations; clubs; volunteer organizations; agency staff; advocacy groups.

DEMOGRAPHIC FACTORS

By looking at such demographic characteristics as population according to age, sex, family size, income, education, and ethnicity, you will not only determine the potential size of the library's market, but its variety as well. Following are ten basic areas to investigate and sources of available data:

Size of population
Population by age and constituent groups
Projections of growth or decline
Ethnic origins
Language
Occupation
Income
Household size
Educational level
Special groups

Sources: U.S. Census; local census; reports of governmental planning and zoning authorities; the community's master plan; surveys of business, industry, and labor organizations; computer modeling for planning from The National Planning Data Corporation's Demographic Database; the Public Library Association's database on communities over 100,000 in population.

COMMUNITY PROFILE ANALYSIS

To frame the analysis of the data you collect on geographic and demographic factors, consider these three questions:

1. Who comprises the population our library is chartered to serve?
2. How do we deliver our programs and services and what influences their delivery?
3. Who are our competitors?

As you make your way through the data, think creatively. Ask yourself how they can be combined to answer the three questions as fully as possible.

Who comprises the population our library is chartered to serve? Review the demographic data that you have collected to answer this question. Data from computer modeling via the online Demographic Database of the National Planning Data Corpo-

---

WORSHEET 4-1   Community Profile: Demographic Characteristics

	1980 #	1980 %	1990* #	1990* %	Projection** 19__ #	Projection** 19__ %
Total population						
White						
Black						
Hispanic						
American Indian						
Asian and Pacific Islander						
Eskimo and Aleut						
Other						

*Or latest figure available from planning studies
**Make projection for the final year of first three-year planning cycle.

ration and other local planning projections will describe what your community looks like now and will help you project what it will look like in the future. Then on Worksheet 4-1, record the size of your community's population by ethnic group, together with the percentage of growth or decline in each group. Since ethnicity and language affect library usage, it is important to detail changes in population along these lines.

WORKSHEET 4-2   Community Profile: Age Groups

	1980			1990*			Projection** 19__	
	#	%	#	%	#	%		
AGE 0–4								
5–12								
13–19								
20–34								
35–55								
56–64								
65+								

*Or latest figure available from planning studies
**Make projection for the final year of first three-year planning cycle.

Next, prepare a breakdown of the total population by age in Worksheet 4-2. The New Age Library made a surprising discovery in their analysis: the community is experiencing a shift in the age of its population. The percentage of residents who are older adults is growing, and all signs indicate that the number of people over age 65 will continue to increase until 2030, when they will comprise nearly 20 percent of the total population.

Education, occupation, and income also are determinants of library use. Studies over time have shown their interrelationship, and all three influence the way in which information is used and requested. Using Worksheet 4-3, you can compile data on your community's educational background. Then on Worksheet 4-4, you can categorize your community by type of occupation. Record current and projected income and gains or losses over the past ten years (derived from the U.S. Decennial Census, then projected into the future) on Worksheet 4-5.

How do we deliver our programs and services and what influences their delivery? How do you get your programs and services to the people they are intended to serve? Library distribution patterns follow a variety of paths: through main and branch locations; on bookmobiles; by way of online services; via interlibrary loan; and books by mail. In addition, your library may have alternate delivery systems for the disabled or for literacy program participants.

Any number of factors can impede or enhance delivery. When the New Age Library looked at its geographic data, it realized that the town's topography had created a barrier to service right at their front door. Flanked on both sides by major traffic thoroughfares, the intersections adjacent to the library are so busy that, while their number is growing, many older adults have stopped coming to the library.

At the same time, cooperative efforts between the community's schools and the library are increasing distribution. Every year the New Age Library joins forces with the town's elementary school media centers to make sure all their students register for library cards. It was during one of these registration periods that the reference librarian and children's librarian were able to confirm an observation with the students' teachers. They noted an influx of children who were staying in the library until they were picked up by their families in the early evening.

Using Worksheet 4-6, consider how your library delivers services and which of the service-setting factors outlined on pages 63–64 significantly affect your delivery systems.

Who are our competitors? A library's competition comes from both likely and unlikely sources. You are providing services during a time when there are more and more small businesses and independent information brokers doing research, social service agencies offering information and referral services, contractors for library services, and even customers who own their own personal computers and buy online time from vendors like DIALOG directly.

Using Worksheet 4-7, identify your competitors and describe their relative strengths and weaknesses. Don't think you are on

WORKSHEET 4-3 Community Profile: Years of School Completed

YEARS	#	1980 %	#	1990* %	#	Projection** 19__ %
Elementary						
1–4						
5–8						
Total						
High School						
1–2						
3–4						
Total						
College						
1–2						
3–4						
Total						
Graduate						
1–2						
3+						
Total						

*Or latest figure available from planning studies

**Make projection for the final year of first three-year planning cycle.

WORKSHEET 4-4 Community Profile: Occupations

	1980			1990*			Projection** 19__	
	#	%	#	%	#	%		

Managerial and
professional specialty

Technical, sales, and
administrative support

Service occupations

Precision production,
craft, and repair

Operators, fabricators,
and laborers

Farming, forestry, and
fishing

*Or latest figure available from planning studies

**Make projection for the final year of first three-year planning cycle.

WORKSHEET 4-5   Community Profile: Income Distribution

	1980			1990*			Projection** 19__	
	#	%	#	%		#		%
Less than $7,500								
$7,500–14,999								
$15,000–19,999								
$20,000–24,999								
$25,000–29,999								
$30,000–34,999								
$35,000–39,999								
$40,000–44,999								
$45,000–49,999								
$50,000–54,999								
$55,000–59,999								
$60,000–64,999								
$65,000–69,999								
$70,000–74,999								
$75,000–99,999								
$100,000 and over								

*Or latest figure available from planning studies
**Make projection for the final year of first three-year planning cycle.

WORKSHEET 4-6   Community Profile: Service Setting Factors Affecting Delivery

What channels of distribution do you use to deliver your programs and services?

Delivery to institutions
Cable TV programs
Radio programs
Computer networks
Bookmobile
   Standard entrance
   Hydraulic lift
Deposit collections
   Neighborhood centers
   Hospitals
   Nursing homes
   Prisons
   Retirement villages
   Housing centers
Books and media by mail
Homebound services
Other _____

Which of the seven service setting factors significantly affect delivery of your programs and services? Indicate those that act as a positive influence and those that act as a negative influence.

	Positive Influence	Negative Influence
History and topography		
Cultural and social organizations		
Educational systems		
Communications networks		
Transportation systems		
Political characteristics		
Community services		

WORKSHEET 4-7   Community Profile: The Competition

Who are your competitors? What are their strengths and weaknesses?

---

a sinking ship if you have compiled a long list. Accept the challenge by doing a competitive scan to figure out their strengths and weaknesses, as well as your own, their advantages over the library in the marketplace, and your advantages over them. It is possible that you'll discover that the service being offered better elsewhere has been a drain on your budget anyway and can be dropped from your menu of programs and services. But it is equally possible that the scan will result in defining your competitive edge so that you can capitalize on it.

When you conduct your competitive scan, you will compare your library with others providing similar programs and services. This will help you think about new ways to compete and make well-grounded decisions about the future. For instance, consider the issue of charging fees for library services. Since cost is the single most important reason customers select a service provider (and it is quite possible that your nonlibrary competitors charge fees), your competitive edge may be close at hand.

Performance Measures

INPUT MEASURES

Definition: Volume of resources coming into the library to support a program or service.

Gather data on: Income (local taxes, capital income, federal funds, state funds, endowments, foundations) and the uses to which it is put (hours open, volumes held, volumes added annually, staff, periodical subscriptions).

OUTPUT MEASURES

Definition: Magnitude of service coming from the library.

Gather data on: Active registration; circulation; turnover rate; in-library use of materials; library visits; materials availability; reference transactions; attendance at programs.

IMPACT MEASURES

Definition: Outcome or consequence of a service or program.

Gather data on: Enhanced skills; behavior (more time spent reading, comfortable use of other libraries, increased visits to the library, borrowing more materials from the library); attitude (desire to read, improved view of self as learner, improved attitude toward learning), satisfaction with program, satisfaction with program facilities, perceived match between program expectations and experience, achievement of personal goals.

It is important to be aware of the offerings of other organizations that might become your competitors in the future. You might even consider joining forces with the competition to bring added value to both your services. For example, the New Age Library and the regional employment service are thinking about teaming up their counselors and librarians to form a Career Center. The employment service head and library director both know that many of the unemployed require more than just referrals to possible jobs. They need access to resources on writing resumes, exploring career options, and interviewing techniques. This is what the center would be equipped to provide.

THE LIBRARY PROFILE

The object of the Library Profile is to determine how responsive your services are to your community by providing a picture of current performance. The Profile is put together through the analysis of data that are derived from input, output, and impact measurement; staff and user surveys; and individual and focus group interviews.

PERFORMANCE MEASUREMENT

Traditionally, performance measurement has been conducted by gathering input and output data. But impact data, which measure the outcome or consequences of a service, are now considered an equally important part of performance measurement.

Your library's own compilations of statistics, as well as those produced by your state library, are among the best sources for input measures. Output measures may require original data collection and analysis. The most comprehensive guide for this is *Output Measures for Public Libraries*.[1] Sources on impact measures are harder to find, since they are only recently getting the attention of the profession. A manual that touches on this is *The Evaluation of Adult Literacy Programs*.[2]

FOCUS GROUPS AND SURVEYS

Focus groups and surveys are often used to amplify performance data. The *focus group* is a relatively new arrival on the library data collection scene. It is a particularly effective, low-cost way of communicating with people who do not use the library. By bringing together individuals who represent your target population, focus groups let you tap into the thoughts, feelings, and

ROLES FOR FOCUS GROUPS

Read the descriptions of library functions listed below. Writer the number which best describes your reaction in each column: 1 = "I think this is a very important role for the library"; 2 = "I think this is somewhat important"; 3 = "I don't think this matters."

Roles	Main Library	Branch

1. Community Activities Center
   A place for meetings; social, cultural, and recreational services.

2. Community Information Center
   A place for information on community organizations, issues, and services; job information; directories; referral networks.

3. Formal Education Support Center
   A place for students in elementary and secondary schools, colleges, community colleges, training programs, and continuing education courses.

4. Independent Learning Center
   A place where individuals set their own learning objectives for education, self-improvement, job-related development, hobbies, cultural interests, etc.

5. Popular Materials Library
   A place which features current, high-demand, high-interest materials, such as video, audio tapes, compact discs, films, paperbacks, and programming on topics of interest to the community.

6. Preschoolers' Door to Learning
   A place for parents and children. Materials on parenting, child care, and child development. Summer reading programs, children's story hours.

7. Reference Library
   A place for on-site and telephone reference/information services; business-related research; government and consumer information; database searching services.

8. Research Library
   A place where scholars conduct research studies; exhaustive information in selected subject areas; customized database searching services.

Focus Group Questions

How often do you use the library?

For what purpose(s) do you use the library?

What benefits do you get from using the library?

What keeps you from using the library?

What is a good library to you?

Do you experience a good library when you come here?

How does your perception compare with your neighbors'?

How familiar are your neighbors with the library's services?

What can we do to make your neighbors more familiar with the library's services?

What are the most important problems the library is facing?

What can be done to improve library service?

What additional services would you like us to offer?

What are the roles you believe the library should play in your community?

attitudes of potential library customers. The sessions usually involve no more than eight people, last about one hour, and are tape-recorded. Transcripts of the answers collected during the interviews, including many direct quotes, can be created from the tapes for analysis.

The focus group interview is far less structured than having an individual sit down and fill out a questionnaire. How a particular question is answered may lead to changes in the order of the questions or in the questions themselves. See the New Age Library's focus group interview schedule on this page.

Focus groups can also help you gather input from users and nonusers alike on the roles they would like to see the library play in the community. *Planning and Role Setting for Public Libraries* provides a full description of possible roles you can adapt to your own focus group efforts.[3] Page 75 lists the roles used by the New Age Library for its focus group.

Questionnaires are the data collection points for *surveys*. They are most successful when targeting library staff and library users, since they can be distributed and collected while the participants are in the library.

A sample User Survey was included at the end of Chapter 3. Two sources for other questionnaires are *A Planning Process for Public Libraries*[4] and *Output Measures for Public Libraries*.[5]

It is important that the questions asked in survey instruments parallel the type of information and data you collect in the Community Profile worksheets, because you will want to compare and contrast potential library customers (Community Profile data) with actual library customers (Library Profile data). You may not always be able to collect quantitative data to make these comparisons. That is where focus group interviews fill in the blanks. You can construct the interview to collect qualitative data for comparison purposes.

All data collection instruments for performance measures, focus groups, or surveys, should be pilot-tested before use and reviewed by the financial planning team to make sure they meet the purpose for which they were intended. If you need help in gathering information, market research firms are one possible source. But be certain the firm you select understands your needs well enough to earn its money.

LIBRARY PROFILE ANALYSIS

To frame the analysis of the data you collected, consider these four questions:

1. Whom does our library serve?

2. What services does it offer and how well is it performing them?
3. What is the comparative level of support for our current programs and services?
4. What promotional activities do we use to reach our current constituents?

Whom does our library serve? The demographic data collected in the Community Profile detailed quantitatively the library's potential audience. Here the actual audience is described. Then the ratio of actual to potential audience can be computed to determine the percentage of the potential audience served, or the level of market penetration:

$$\frac{\text{Actual}}{\text{Potential}} = \% \text{ population served (market penetration)}$$

You can compute this ratio on Worksheet 4-8 using the statistics from your user survey and those gathered in the Community Profile on population. For example, if the Community Profile showed that 12 percent of the total population is between the ages of five and thirteen, compare that with the data showing percentage of users between the age of five and thirteen as determined by the user survey.

What services does the library currently offer and how well is it performing them? By using the checklist on Worksheet 4-9, which is adapted from *Adult Services an Enduring Focus for Public Libraries*, indicate which services your library is currently offering.[6]

Your compilations of input, output, and impact data will show you how well you are providing services. Using state library data to position your library on input vis-à-vis other libraries with similar characteristics, complete Worksheet 4-10.

The output measure most commonly computed is circulation. You can also compare it on Worksheet 4-10. Other output measures you can consider collecting include numbers of: registered borrowers, library visits, reference transactions, and program attendance.

If you conduct a user survey, consider asking questions about materials' availability by subject, author, title, and judgment of collection adequacy.

Impact data can provide vital information here as well. They rely on information collection primarily through interviews and

WORKSHEET 4-8 Library Profile: Who Does Our Library Serve?

Data for Potential Customers can be retrieved from Worksheets 4-1 through 4-5.
Data for Actual Customers will come from your user surveys.

	Potential Customers	Actual Customers	Market Penetration*
Total population			
White			
Black			
Hispanic			
American Indian			
Asian and Pacific Islander			
Eskimo and Aleut			
Other			
Age			
0–4			
5–12			
13–19			
20–34			
35–55			
56–64			
65+			
Education Elementary 1–4			
5–8			
High School 1–2			
3–4			
College 1–2			
3–4			
Graduate 1–2			
3+			

* $\dfrac{\text{Actual}}{\text{Potential}}$ = % of Population

WORKSHEET 4-8 (Continued)

	Potential Customers	Actual Customers	Market Penetration*

Occupation
  Managerial and
    Professional specialty			

Technical, sales, and administrative support			
Service occupations			
Precision production, craft, and repair			
Operators, fabricators, and laborers			
Farming, forestry, and fishing			
Income Less than $7,500			
$7,500–14,999			
$15,000–19,999			
$20,000–24,999			
$25,000–29,999			
$30,000–34,999			
$35,000–39,999			
$40,000–44,999			
$45,000–49,999			
$50,000–54,999			
$55,000–59,999			
$60,000–64,999			
$65,000–69,999			
$70,000–74,999			
$75,000–99,999			
$100,000 and over			

* $\dfrac{\text{Actual}}{\text{Potential}}$ = % population served (market penetration)

WORKSHEET 4-9   Library Profile—Checklist of Library Services

Reference and Other General Services
   Information and referral
   Municipal information service
   Information on demand
   Information from online databases
   Job information centers
   Oral history
   Genealogy
   Local history
   Bibliotherapy
   Lifelong learning
      Basic education classes
      Graduate equivalency diploma classes
      English as a second language classes
      Literacy programs
      Independent learning programs
      Education brokering
      Instruction on library use
   Reading lists and bibliographies
   Other _____

Resources
   Books
   Periodicals
   Large-print books
   Talking books
   Magnifying devices
   Ethnic material
   Foreign-language material
   Films
   Audio recordings
   Videocassettes
   Ceiling projectors
   Page turners
   Kurzweil reading machines
   Telecommunications for the deaf
   Closed-captioned viewing adaptors
   Other _____

Internal Programs
   Clubs
   Films
   Live artists
   Lectures
   Book talks
   Discussion groups
   Exhibits
      Art
      Artifacts
      Exhibits of library materials

WORKSHEET 4-9 *Continued*

Programs for special groups
 Businesspersons
 Handicapped
 Genealogists
 Job seekers
 Older adults
 Parents
 Minorities
 Other _____

Other Programs Offered Outside the Library
 Clubs
 Films
 Live artists
 Lectures
 Book talks
 Discussion groups
 Other _____

Computing Services
 Micros available for inhouse use
 Circulating micros
 Other _____

Computing Services
 Micros available for inhouse use
 Circulating micros
 Other _____

Circulation Services
 Books to individuals
 Books in multiple copies to groups
 Musical records
 Spoken records
 Musical tapes
 Films
 Videocassettes
 Audiovisual equipment
  In-library use
  Out-of-library use
  Other _____

Support Services
 Meeting or conference room space
 Photocopy machines
 Other _____

WORKSHEET 4-10 Library Profile: Comparative Statistics

	Your Library	Library I	Library II
Population served			
Full-time Employees			
Professional Librarians			
Volumes Owned Year End			
Volumes Added During Year			
Volumes per Capita			
Periodical Subscription			
Circulation			
Hours Open			
Total Income			
Total Expenditures			

surveys that question users of a service or participants in a program about their expectations and perceptions of the benefits.

What is the comparative level of support for current programs and services? One way to approach this question is to compare total library resources with resources committed to particular service groups. The comparison will show whether or not the level of support is adequate to serve the large and/or growing populations you found when you completed the Community Profile. For example, the New Age Library's financial planning team used its Library Profile to determine how resources were being deployed to support children's and older adult services. The planning team wanted to see if the current level of support is sufficient in view of the growth trends in the older adult population and in the number of children using the library. Complete the horizontal grid on Worksheet 4-11 with the headings shown or with your choice of services and supply the appropriate data.

What promotional activities do we use to reach our current constituents? Through which media does your library let the community know about its services? Do you:

- arrange to have articles about the library published in local newspapers, magazines, and newsletters?
- use public access radio and television to advertise your programs and services?
- have a Friends of the Library group?
- do direct mail promotions to let your community know about new arrivals or services?
- have posters celebrating the library displayed prominently throughout the community?
- give talks about library services at meetings, organizations, and points of service for other agencies?
- go from door-to-door in targeted neighborhoods?
- conduct telemarketing?
- advertise services on billboards and bus cards?
- collect testimonials to attract more users from target groups?

Focus group interviews and user surveys will supply data on the sources the library's current audience turns to for information on library services. Using Worksheet 4-12, check the promotional activities you use. Then note those indicated by focus group participants.

WORKSHEET 4-11   Library Profile: Current Level of Support

	Older Adult Services		Adult Services		Young Adult Services		Children Services		Total	
	$	% Total	$	% Total	$	% Total	$	% Total	$	% Total
Income										
Endowments										
Grants										
Local support										
Capital funds										
Other										
Expenditures										
Salaries & wages										
Materials										
Per capita expenditure										
Other										
Staff										
Professional										
Full-time										
Full-time equivalent (F.T.E.)										
Volunteer										
Other										
Volumes & Media										
Owned year end										
Purchased during year										
Periodical subscriptions										
Other										
Circulation										
Current year										
Change last year										
Facilities										
Square feet of building space										
Number of buildings										

WORKSHEET 4-12   Library Profile: Checklist of Promotional Activities

What promotional activities do we use to reach our current customers?

	Used by Library*	Used by Participants**
Newspapers, magazines, newsletters		
Radio		
Television		
Computer networks		
Friends of the Library		
Direct mail		
Posters		
Presentations to community groups		
Door-to-door solicitations		
Telemarketing		
Billboards		
Business cards		
Testimonials		
Other		

*Check off those used by library.

**Write in which group provided information about the source during the focus group session, e.g., small-business owner, student, lawyer, factory worker, etc.

LOOKING INTO THE FUTURE

Comparing the information gathered in the Community Profile (the potential audience) with the information gathered in the Library Profile (the actual audience) provides a measure of your library's current responsiveness. But what about tomorrow? Some questions to consider that will help you decide upon new directions for the future include:

1. What is our potential for recruiting new customers?
2. What new services should we consider providing to new customers?
3. What new channels of distribution will we need to deliver services and programs to new customers?
4. What promotional activities will we add to reach new customers?

What is our potential for recruiting new customers? In the Community Profile you described the potential population your library is chartered to serve. In the Library Profile you determined the actual population you are serving and compared the two. Those unserved comprise a potential source of new library customers. Now you are ready to pinpoint the populations you aren't attracting at all or in sufficient numbers. Use Worksheet 4-13 for these calculations.

What new services should we consider providing to new customers? You prepared a list of services the library currently offers on Worksheet 4-9. Consider the services that are not part of your library's repertoire. What did your focus group interviews reveal about services that might attract new customers to the library? On Worksheet 4-14, compile a list of services you want to consider.

What new channels of distribution will we need to deliver services and programs to new customers? How will you deliver programs and services to the potential customer groups you have identified? Focus group interviews will provide some answers. It is possible that since they may not be traditional library users, your usual modes of delivery may not be sufficient to meet their needs. Use Worksheet 4-15 to compile a list of channels of distribution you think will meet the needs of new customers. Go back to your Community Profile. Reconsider the channels of dis-

WORKSHEET 4-13   Potential Customers

	Market Penetration (% population served*)	%** Unserved
Total population		
White		
Black		
Hispanic		
American Indian		
Asian and Pacific Islander		
Eskimo and Aleut		
Other		
Age		
0–4		
5–12		
13–19		
20–34		
35–55		
55–65		
65+		
Education		
Elementary		
1–4		
5–8		
High School		
1–2		
3–4		
College		
1–2		
3–4		
Graduate		
1–2		
3+		
Occupation		
Managerial and professional specialty		
Technical, sales and administrative support		
Service occupations		
Precision production, craft, and repair		
Operators, fabricators, and laborers		
Farming, forestry, and fishing		

*From Worksheet 4-8.
**% unserved = 100% – % population served.

WORKSHEET 4-13 (Continued)

Income	Market Penetration (% population served*)	%** Unserved
Less than $7,500		
$7,500–14,999		
$15,000–19,999		
$20,000–24,999		
$25,000–29,999		
$30,000–34,999		
$35,000–39,999		
$40,000–44,999		
$45,000–49,999		
$50,000–54,999		
$55,000–59,999		
$60,000–64,999		
$65,000–69,999		
$70,000–74,999		
$75,000–99,999		
$100,000 and over		

*From Worksheet 4-8.

**% unserved = 100% – % population served.

WORKSHEET 4-14 New Services for Potential Customers

What new services do we want to provide to attract potential customers?

1. _____
   _____
   _____

2. _____
   _____
   _____

3. _____
   _____
   _____

4. _____
   _____
   _____

5. _____
   _____
   _____

tribution. Which will you continue to capitalize on? Which will you add that you haven't yet used? Also, review the service-setting factors: Which positive influences will you continue to exploit? Which negative influences will you work to overcome?

What promotional activities will we add to reach new customers? Return to Worksheet 4-12 and consider those activities not used which data indicate may be useful for reaching new customers. The information you collected from surveys and focus group interviews should have pointed out ways to make target audiences more familiar with the library's services. On Worksheet 4-16 list those promotional outlets overlooked by the library that are used by the potential customers the library seeks to reach.

When you have completed this analysis, you will have moved from a review of the status of the library's current and future

WORKSHEET 4-15   New Channels of Distribution

Which channels of distribution not currently in use by the library could meet the needs of new customers?

Delivery to institutions
Cable TV programs
Radio programs
Computer networks
Bookmobile
   Standard entrance
   Hydraulic lift
Deposit collections
   Neighborhood centers
   Hospitals
   Nursing homes
   Prisons
   Retirement villages
   Housing centers
Books and media by mail
Homebound services
Other _____

_____

_____

_____

Which service setting factors exerting a positive influence on delivery will you continue to exploit? How?

Which service setting factors exerting a negative influence on delivery will you work to overcome? How?

WORKSHEET 4-16
New Promotions

What types of promotional
outlets will we use to
reach our new customers?

Newspapers,
   magazines,
     newsletters
Radio
Television
Computer networks
Friends of the Library
Direct mail
Posters
Presentations to
community
    groups
Door-to-door solicitations
Telemarketing
Billboards
Bus cards
Testimonials
Other _____

1. _____

2. _____

3. _____

4. _____

audiences and services to a course for the future and the means to promote that course.

MOVING FORWARD

You have collected a good amount of data through the Community and Library Profiles that should give you a strong picture of your organization, how it fits into the community it serves, how well it is serving its current customers, and whether there are new audiences to recruit and introduce to what your library has to offer. You now should be able to answer the question, "How well are we doing?" and determine whether and where there is room for improved or additional programs and services in the future.

A marketing orientation holds that the main task of the fully responsive library is to determine the needs and wants of its target markets and to satisfy them through the design, communication, and delivery of appropriate and competitive services. Now that you have completed your market analysis, let's return to where we began this chapter: with your financial planning team considering how responsive your library is to your community.

Our library is:
____ responsive
____ highly responsive
____ fully responsive

Now ask yourselves how responsive you want it to be in the future.

In the future, we want our library to be:
____ responsive
____ highly responsive
____ fully responsive

ENDNOTES

1. Nancy VanHouse, Mary Jo Lynch, Charles R. McClure, Douglas L. Zweizig, and Eleanor Jo Rodger, *Output Measures for Public Libraries*, 2nd ed.
(Chicago: American Library Association, 1987), 15–27.
2. Douglas L. Zweizig, Debra Wilcox Johnson, and Jane B. Robbins, *Evaluation of Adult Literacy Programs* (Chicago: American Library Association, 1990), 37–43.
3. Charles R. McClure, Amy Owen, Douglas L. Zweizig, Mary Jo Lynch, and
Nancy A. VanHouse, *Planning and Role Setting for Public Libraries* (Chicago: American Library Association, 1987), 30–42.
4. Vernon E. Palmour, Marcia C. Bellassai, and Nancy V. DeWath, *A Planning
Process for Public Libraries* (Chicago: American Library Association,
1980), 217–227.
5. VanHouse, 56–62.
6. Kathleen M. Heim, and Danny P. Wallace, eds., *Adult Services: An Enduring Focus for Public Libraries* (Chicago: American Library Association,
1990), 53–165.

PART THREE

SETTING THE COURSE

5 ASSUMPTIONS, GOALS, AND OBJECTIVES

We began this book by discussing your library's overall mission, goals, and objectives and their role in the financial planning process. Now it is time to add *financial goals and objectives* to the picture.

The work you completed in Chapters 2, 3, and 4 has provided you with a diagnosis of your library's finances, situation, and markets. You questioned its operations, services, and programs and identified the internal and external factors that affect them. You also collected a wide array of data to verify your diagnosis. Now it's time to turn your attention to the development of financial goals and objectives, which will act as milestones in the financial planning process by setting priorities for action. Three steps will help you create those goals and objectives.

The WOTS Up? Formula

Weakness (−): lack of strength; inability to sustain or exert pressure; inability to resist force or function properly.

Opportunity (+): a favorable juncture of circumstances; a good chance for advancement or progress.

Threat (−): a warning or sign; an indication of something pending.

Strength (+): the quality of being strong; incorporating solidity and toughness; vigor of expression.

STEP 1

IDENTIFY STRENGTHS AND WEAKNESSES, OPPORTUNITIES AND THREATS

The first step is to confront what your library has going for it and what is working against it. A classic *WOTS Up?* grid will help you accomplish this. The formula lets you look at your library's Weaknesses, Opportunities, Threats, and Strengths. The weaknesses and threats are, of course, negatives; the strengths and opportunities are positives.

Consider the circumstances of the New Age Library. The financial planning team's review of the library's fiscal status, along with the situation and market analyses, revealed some disturbing aspects of the library's operations. To clearly distinguish what they have going for them and what is working against them, the New Age Library financial planning team constructed a *WOTS Up?* grid and labeled each factor as a weakness, opportunity, threat, or strength. Figure 5-1 shows the results.

The fiscal status review revealed a troublesome trend. Over the years spending has increased at a more rapid rate than income. Also, financial ratios, although adequate, are losing ground.

In the situation analysis, the financial planning team finds that the local economic downturn is mirroring the broader national picture. On the plus side, the recent city council election just added a pro-library council member after years of inadequate represen-

FIGURE 5-1   WOTS UP? Grid

	Weakness (−)	Opportunity (+)	Threat (−)	Strength (+)
Factors in Fiscal Status	Economic downturn		Trend—expenditures are out-pacing income. Ratios losing ground	
Factors in Situation Analysis	Low productivity in some areas	Can improve operating efficiencies		Cultivate support of new council member
Factors in Market Analysis	Unmet users: 1. Latch key children 2. Unemployed 3. Older adults	Initiate new programs for unmet users		

tation. Internally, a series of productivity studies have pinpointed low levels of efficiency in several of the library's service units. If corrected, they should lead to staff members being freed up for direct service to improve the library's responsiveness.

Finally, the market analysis uncovered three growing target audiences: latchkey children, the unemployed, and older adults.

So, *WOTS Up?* at the New Age Library? The team has identified three weaknesses: low productivity, the economic downturn, and three user groups with unmet needs. At the same time, the team considers both the low productivity and unmet needs opportunities. They know that low productivity can be turned around. And they see great opportunities for reorganization and collaboration, for example initiating a career center and providing innovative intergenerational programming, in responding to the needs of the unemployed, latchkey children, and older adults.

The team considers the fact that expenditures are increasing more rapidly than income to be the major threat, but believes the new council member can be influential in reversing this trend.

Now on Worksheet 5-1 you can apply the *WOTS Up?* formula to your library, using all of the material you collected and analyzed from Chapters 2, 3, and 4. Label as a weakness, opportunity, threat, and/or strength the factors you identified as a result of your fiscal status inquiry and situation and market analyses. Take the time now to sort through the data and write your initial analysis in the grid boxes. You can always adjust and refine the material later. The definitions at the beginning of the chapter will help you distinguish the positives from the negatives.

ASSUMPTIONS
Assumptions are judgment statements made by the financial planning team about possible occurrences in the future. Drawn from the data compiled in the fiscal, situation, and market analyses, they enable the team to assess potential risks the library could face in the future. And they can lead to actions that could reduce those risks.

STEP 2

SET ASSUMPTIONS
By looking at the evidence you've gathered in the *WOTS Up?* grid—which describes the present—you can begin to make assumptions about the future. The assumptions you make should be focused on what you consider critical to the library's development. They are not meant to encompass everything you have found in the data you collected. You will want to consider what factors in the library's internal and external environment will influence *most* the course of the financial plan. The assumptions should apply to the three-year financial planning period. The numbers you present later in your budgetary forecasts will have

WORKSHEET 5-1   WOTS UP? Grid

	Weakness	Opportunity	Threat	Strength
Factors in Fiscal Status				
Factors in Situation Analysis				
Factors in Market Analysis				

little meaning unless you clearly and precisely set out the assumptions upon which you built them.

All assumptions are based on an underlying premise. Nothing will occur that will sway the data in another direction. In other words, if inflation has been tracked in the situation analysis and the data reveal that it has stayed relatively constant, you will extrapolate that inflation will continue over the next three years. If, however, inflation has been playing roller coaster over the country's economy, your assumptions must take that into account.

ASSUMPTIONS DERIVED FROM FINANCIAL STATUS

Your assumptions here will be derived from such information as the past three years' expenditures, income, and ratios. Based on how you complete the *WOTS Up?* grid, your assumptions will attempt to predict movement over the next three years.

When the New Age Library began setting assumptions, it came up with three:

1. Income from traditional sources will show little growth during the financial planning period.
2. Expenditures will outpace income.
3. The library will need new sources of income.

ASSUMPTIONS DERIVED FROM SITUATION ANALYSIS

Your assumptions here will be derived from the external and internal factors impacting on the library environment. Here are two set by the New Age Library's financial planning team:

External assumption: The economic downturn is not likely to reverse itself over the next three years.

Internal assumption: Productivity can be increased through an analysis of targeted library operations.

ASSUMPTIONS DERIVED FROM MARKET ANALYSIS

Your financial planning team will want to examine a variety of market issues in order to zero in on the most crucial (e.g., current customers, competition, promotional activities, and channels of distribution).

One assumption set by the New Age Library was:

WORKSHEET 5-2   Setting Assumptions

Assumptions about the library's fiscal status

1. _____   3. _____
   _____   _____
2. _____   4. _____
   _____   _____

Assumptions about the library's external and internal situation

External   *Internal*

1. _____   1. _____
   _____   _____
2. _____   2. _____
   _____   _____
3. _____   3. _____
   _____   _____

Assumptions about the library's market

1. _____   3. _____
   _____   _____
2. _____   4. _____
   _____   _____

Assumption: Market penetration can be increased in three groups—latchkey children, the unemployed, and older adults.

On Worksheet 5-2, sketch out the assumptions you feel best represent your library's markets. Use the *WOTS Up?* grid to help you formulate them. Remember, you can't take on every problem or opportunity that shows up on the grid in one year. You have to decide which are the most important influences on your library, set them in priority order, and phase them into the three-year financial plan.

STEP 3

SET FINANCIAL GOALS AND OBJECTIVES

Goals and objectives reflect the problems you will face and the changes you hope to effect. By projecting into the future, you will be able to create a description of the library three years from now. Your assumptions are predictions, the basis for formulating your financial goals and objectives if current conditions continue on a steady course. Goals and objectives are set to overcome assumptions about the future that would portend adverse conditions for the library.

Always keep in mind the difference between your library's financial goals and objectives and its overall goals and objectives. While the library's general goals and objectives are concerned with programs, services, and staff development, its *financial* goals and objectives are concerned with the funding to provide the resources to accomplish them.

Your financial goals are strategic, long-range, and visionary. They guide your library toward where you want to be at the end of the financial planning period.

Your financial objectives are tactical and measurable; they are focused on what is to be produced monetarily. They set the course for how you will move forward in response to your financial goals. An objective that states that a library will increase by 10 percent the amount of income generated through grants by the end of the fiscal year supplies clearly quantifiable evidence of whether or not the fiscal target is achieved. A second objective, stating that by the end of the fiscal year the library will have completed its financial plan as a prospectus to present to foundations, also supplies evidence—the existence of the plan itself.

Your financial objectives are set within a specific time frame: a date for planning and a date for implementation. They often

THREE QUESTIONS YOU MUST ANSWER

1. What is your financial objective?
2. How will you measure success?
3. How long will it take?

specify accountability by indicating who is responsible for accomplishing them—one person or an entire department.

When writing financial goals and objectives, never lose sight of the fact that the overall driving forces are the library's *general* goals and objectives. The financial goals and objectives cannot conflict with them. Take, for example, a library that has as one of its general goals to provide free information services, and has as one of its financial goals to increase its income by 10 percent. Can it consider charging a fee for online database searches? Not without considerable conflict. Although this is in line with the financial goal, it is out of line with the library's general goal.

When the New Age Library began writing its financial goals and objectives, it focused first on the assumptions it made about its financial status: that income will show little growth during the financial planning period; that expenditures will continue to grow at the current pace; and that the library needs new sources of income.

And so, their first goal is as follows:

Goal: To protect the library from future loss of revenue.

To help meet this goal, the library devised two objectives:

Objective: Retain at least two percent of the local government's total appropriation for community services over the next three years.

Objective: Within six months, appoint a development officer who will begin to analyze sources of income and prepare a scheduled plan to diversify.

Since the trend of expenditures outpacing income was a bad sign for the long term, protecting the library from loss of revenue in a time of economic downturn was a natural goal to set. Unless they stop this trend, service will erode. That's why the library's first objective is to retain its current share of local tax revenues— its primary source of support. The library just can't do with a reduction, so it is going to make sure the new council member understands and helps the library make its case for continued, if not additional, support.

The second objective, to appoint a development officer who will set the course for diversification of income sources, is in response to the library's heavy reliance on tax revenues. The library realizes it needs alternate sources to remain stable—if not grow.

The New Age Library's second financial goal was written in response to the assumptions derived from the situation analysis—that cost efficiencies could be realized through an analysis of current library operations. The goal is:

Goal: To maximize the use of library resources.

And the two objectives established to reach that goal are:

Objective: Within one year, reduce costs for continuing services at least two percent by addressing inefficiencies uncovered in productivity studies.

Objective: Review operations to stabilize or reduce costs another one percent within two years.

The financial planning team decided that a global statement addressing the problems inherent in operating in an environment of continuing low resources was important. The library's ability to introduce new services, while keeping those that continue to have value for the community, would be dependent not only on retaining the library's share of local tax revenue and diversifying sources of income, but also on streamlining continued operations so that resources could be allocated to crucial new services.

The financial planning team conducted a series of productivity studies as part of its situation analysis. Several inefficiencies in work distribution indicated that costs could be reduced and more services could be produced with the same amount of resources if these inefficiencies were eliminated.

The financial planning team also initiated a series of cost-accounting operations to reduce costs. For instance, they conducted a cost analysis to determine a fair price for services supplied to them by contractors. In several cases, they were able to create competition among suppliers who, as a result, reduced prices.

The team also established one point of delivery for the library and its branches, which not only reduced suppliers' costs, but their prices. Where feasible, the library began ordering in larger and more economical quantities. This also lowered costs. Finally, they negotiated longer contracts at lower prices. All in all, the library set out to pay no more than absolutely necessary for the services they purchased.

With their two goals and four objectives in place, the financial planning team looked ahead with excitement. They had already identified the needs of latchkey children, the unemployed, and older adults as opportunities. By meeting the goals of increasing efficiency and diversifying resources—and maintaining their share of the tax pie—growth itself seemed an opportunity. And so, the New Age Library set as a third financial goal:

Goal: To provide for the library's continued financial growth.

The financial planning team set the following objectives to meet this goal:

Objective: Over the next two years, realize further internal savings of two percent, and reorganize library service provision by joining forces with other service agencies to deliver library services to newly discovered audiences.

Objective: Over the next three years, add at least five percent each year to the library's total income from new funding sources.

Now it's your turn. With your library's general goals and objectives and your assumptions about the future in hand, you are ready to set your library's *financial* goals and objectives on Worksheet 5-3. They will address your library's biggest threats and weaknesses and make the most of its opportunities and strengths.

Create at least one financial goal and, for each goal, set at least two objectives. Don't forget to include for each objective the intended result, a time frame, and who is responsible for meeting the objective.

Goal and objective setting—as well as assumption making—all are very creative actions. There are limitless possibilities—the words on the *WOTS Up?* grid are just the beginning. The assumptions help you start thinking about possibilities.

Your financial goals and objectives are the heart of the financial plan. As such, don't be surprised by the amount of time and effort required to get them just right. Expect to have many planning sessions, and allow time in between for many drafts and reviews of the measures and targets.

WORKSHEET 5-3   Setting Financial Goals and Objectives

Problem Identification

1. Looking at the WOTS UP? grid, list below all the weaknesses, opportunities, threats, and strengths:

Weakness	Opportunity	Threat	Strength
_____	_____	_____	_____
_____	_____	_____	_____
_____	_____	_____	_____
_____	_____	_____	_____
_____	_____	_____	_____
_____	_____	_____	_____
_____	_____	_____	_____
_____	_____	_____	_____
_____	_____	_____	_____
_____	_____	_____	_____
_____	_____	_____	_____
_____	_____	_____	_____
_____	_____	_____	_____
_____	_____	_____	_____
_____	_____	_____	_____
_____	_____	_____	_____
_____	_____	_____	_____

Consider each factor closely. For every weakness and threat look for potential responses to overcome them from the list of opportunities and strengths. Then, rank each list in priority order: Number 1 should receive the earliest attention.

WORKSHEET 5-3 *Continued*

2. Setting assumptions

   (Refer to assumptions on Worksheet 5-2.)

   _____

   _____

   _____

   _____

   _____

   _____

   _____

   _____

   _____

3. Setting goals

   Set at least one financial goal for each of the factors you determined to be a priority.

   _____

   _____

   _____

   _____

   _____

   _____

   _____

   _____

   _____

WORKSHEET 5-3 *Continued*

4. Setting objectives

   Set at least two financial objectives for each goal listed above. Include in each objective's statement the particular outcome, measure of achievement, and a time frame. If you wish, add who is responsible for taking action.

   _____

   _____

   _____

   _____

   _____

   _____

   _____

   _____

   _____

   _____

   _____

   _____

   _____

Estimated Start-Up Costs for the Career Center

Direct Costs

Personnel

  Librarian

50% at $35,000	$17,650
Benefits at 24%	4,236
Clerical Support	
25% at $18,000	4,500
Social Security	350
Total Labor Costs	$26,736
Other Direct Costs	
Materials	5,000
Supplies	550
Telephone	350
Postage	250
Equipment	3,000
Total Direct Costs	35,886
Indirect Cost (Rate at 3%*)	1,077
Total Start-Up Costs	$36,963
Library's Actual Costs at 2/3	$24,642

*Indirect Cost Rate = $\dfrac{\$26{,}736 \text{ Direct Labor Costs for the Center}}{\$892{,}189 \text{ Direct Labor Costs for Adult Services}}$

CREATING BUDGETARY FORECASTS

Too frequently, annual budgeting leads to short-term thinking. One of the main objectives of financial planning is to gain fiscal control of the library over the long haul. That's why at this point you are going to take your current operating budget and create a forecast for each of the three years of your financial plan, indicating the money needed to support the services—both continuing and new—you have projected over the planning cycle. Libraries anticipating a major purchase within the three years—such as land, equipment, building construction or reconstruction, or a computer system—will have to forecast capital expenditures as well.

During budgetary forecasting, you will decide which objectives can be accomplished in the coming year and which will have to be reserved for each of the two succeeding years. In fact, the forecasts are used to monitor how the library is conforming to its planned schedule of expenditures. They are regularly compared to the operating budget over the three-year planning cycle and adjusted as needed to reflect the library's evolving fiscal reality. Forecasts also act as a means of communicating with the financial decision makers of your parent organization and alerting them early on to your future financial requirements.

PRICING SERVICES

In order to forecast budgetary needs, costs must be estimated for any new services you want to initiate. As mentioned in Chapter 3, Philip Rosenberg's *Cost Finding* presents a model for calculating exact costs.[1] Since this can be a time-consuming process, the four-step model suggested here will provide you with cost estimates which, for the purpose of the financial plan, are sufficient.

STEP 1: DETERMINE THE COST OF TIME

Calculate the cost of time by taking the annual salaries of the staff and prorate them in proportion to the total time given over to the task. Add to that the cost of benefits, also prorated in proportion to time. See the box on page 108, which shows how the New Age Library estimated the start-up costs for the Career Center they want to open with the regional employment center. You'll see that they are planning for one half-time librarian and one quarter-time clerical worker. Benefits for the librarian are computed at 24 percent; only Social Security is included for the clerical support, since she will work less than 20 hours a week.

STEP 2: RECORD DIRECT COSTS

Direct costs are those easily attributable to a specific service, like the personnel, materials, equipment, telephone, postage, and supplies for the New Age Library's Career Center.

STEP 3: ESTIMATE INDIRECT COSTS

Indirect costs are those costs that cannot be readily identified with and charged to a specific service, but are necessary to the performance of various services. Administration, finance/accounting, maintenance, utilities, and security are generally considered indirect costs.

Calculating indirect costs begins by determining the indirect cost rate using the following formula:

$$\frac{\text{Service Unit's Direct Labor Costs}}{\text{Total Direct Labor Costs}} = \text{Indirect Rate}$$

For the Career Center:

$$\frac{26,736}{892,189} = .03$$

The total for all direct costs—materials, supplies, telephone, postage, and equipment plus total labor costs—is multiplied by the indirect rate, which gives you the estimate of indirect costs ($35,886 × .03 = $1,077).

STEP 4: DETERMINE ACTUAL SERVICE COSTS

Direct and indirect costs are added to estimate the total actual start-up costs ($35,886 + $1,077 = $36,963). In this case, since the regional employment office has agreed to finance one-third the cost, the actual cost to the library is $24,642.

With its costs analysis in hand, the New Age Library was ready to set new service priorities. Because of the community's high unemployment rate, and since they are sharing the costs and resources necessary for the start-up and ongoing operation of the Career Center with the regional employment service, the financial planning team opted to proceed with the Career Center immediately. They projected initiating the center—and adding a Development Officer—in Year 1. Services to latchkey children would begin in Year 2, and services to older adults in Year 3.

SELECTING A BUDGET FORMAT

With costs for continuing services revealed through productivity studies and cost analyses—and with funding requirements projected for all new services—you are ready to forecast your library's expenditures for the three-year financial planning period using one of the formats presented below.

The budget format you select should be the one you apply to the preparation of your forecasts. Even though you may be using the line-item format now, there are three others from which to choose: program, performance, and zero-base (ZBB). They represent building blocks in a hierarchy that supplies an increasingly complete picture of the costs to provide service.

The program format links library service to fiscal requests. The performance format contains all of the information found in the program format and adds unit costs. The ZBB, which includes the information gathered for the first two, starts with the assumption that not all current programs are worthy of continued funding and ends with a priority ranking of services. Information to help you select the forecasting and budgeting format right for your library is developed here through examples based on the New Age Library.

LINE-ITEM FORMAT

The line-item approach focuses on expenditures. It shows in the aggregate what is going to be spent in a particular year. It assumes that all categories of expenditures made one year must be continued in the next, and that all activities included last year are not only essential but are performed in the most cost-effective manner. For each year's budgetary forecast, costs are adjusted simply to reflect inflation. If a higher inflationary factor is identified as affecting a specific item on a line, (increased postal rates for instance), it is passed on to that particular line item. Otherwise, the same inflationary factor is applied to all items. All line items are considered continually funded, with nothing qualifying their use or success.

When a new program is initiated, costs are dispersed among the line items applicable to that program. Take the New Age Library's joint venture with the regional employment service. With the line-item format, there is no place where the operating costs for the Career Center are brought together. Instead, the library estimates for start-up and ongoing funding will be dispersed among the items already listed. There is no way to distinguish the costs for this new program from other ongoing programs.

The current operating budget of the New Age Library, in Figure 6-1, demonstrates the line-item format. It includes such broad categories as personnel, benefits, materials, supplies, communication, equipment, equipment maintenance, conferences and dues, contracted services, and staff development.

Looking at this format, you can see that there is no way to tell whether increases are the result of new programs or services, since it's impossible to associate requests with the specific costs of supplying a service. The emphasis is on the commodities to be purchased. The lines are clearly defined, which permits easier accounting. However, it does not stress the library's goal of service to the community.

THE PROGRAM FORMAT

Here each service unit budgets its expenditures in response to its service goals and objectives, incorporating these goals and objectives as an integral part of the financial planning process. If, for example, the New Age Library constructed its current year budget for adult services in the program format, as shown in Figure 6-2, that program's goals and objectives would precede the calculated expenditures: personnel, materials, and operating costs:

Goal: To provide reference, readers advisory, and I & R services, materials, and programming for the potential and current adult customers in the community.

Objective: Provide timely, accurate responses to telephone and walk-in queries via print, nonprint, and electronic sources.

Goal: To collaborate with other community agencies to implement the Career Center to assist the unemployed and other job seekers.

Objective: Maintain an up-to-date database of community information and agencies for referral (I & R).

Unlike the line-item format, the same percentage increase is not automatically affixed to each line of last year's figures. The emphasis is on ensuring that allocations are related to the level of services provided. Funding is reviewed, deleted, replaced, or shifted as library programs change.

FIGURE 6-1   Current Year Line-Item Operating Budget

New Age Library

Account Code	Category	Projected Expenditure
100300	Personnel	
100301	Full-time	600,765
100302	Part-time	117,933
100303	Overtime	8,817
200300	Benefits	
200301	Social Security	55,654
200302	Pension	60,959
200303	Health Insurance	48,061
	TOTAL PERSONNEL	$892,189
300300	Materials	
300301	Books	188,086
300302	Periodicals	49,913
300303	Databases	23,343
300304	Documents	5,761
300305	Media	26,210
	TOTAL MATERIALS	$293,313
400300	Supplies	
400301	Office	5,618
400302	Computer	3,413

FIGURE 6-1 (*Continued*)

500300	Communications	
500301	Postage	13,482
500302	Telephone	6,815
500303	Datalines	14,445
600300	Memberships and Conferences	
600301	Dues	3,000
600302	Conference	1,095
700300	Staff Development	
700301	Travel	5,000
700302	Other	500
800300	Contracted Services	
800301	Programming	8,250
800302	Utilities	10,510
900300	Equipment and Repairs	
900301	Minor Equipment	500
900302	General Maintenance	1,250
900303	Van Costs	2,000
900304	Insurance	1,500
900205	Repairs	<u>1,000</u>
	TOTAL OPERATING	$78,378
	GRAND TOTAL	<u>$1,263,880</u>

FIGURE 6-2   Current Program Budget Adult Services

New Age Library

Account Code	Category	Adult Services	Information and Programming Services	Circulation Services	Interlibrary Loan	Nonprint Services
100300	Personnel					
100301	Full-time	310,705	195,705	70,000	27,000	18,000
100302	Part-time	51,958	8,378	31,540	6,020	6,020
100303	Overtime	4,097	1,087	3,010	—	—
200300	Benefits					
200301	Social Security	28,057	15,695	7,998	2,526	1,838
200302	Pension	31,480	19,679	7,301	2,700	1,800
200303	Health Insurance	24,856	15,656	5,600	2,160	1,440
	TOTAL PERSONNEL	$451,153	256,200	125,449	40,406	29,098
300300	Materials					
300301	Books	119,350	45,623	73,107	—	620
300302	Periodicals	46,552	17,507	28,735	—	310
300303	Databases	19,191	14,000	1,507	2,611	1,073
300304	Documents	5,069	5,069	—	—	—
300305	Media	26,210	—	—	—	26,210
	TOTAL MATERIALS	$216,372	82,199	103,349	2,611	28,213
400300	Supplies					
400301	Office	2,074	507	976	370	221
400302	Computer	1,938	752	499	125	562

FIGURE 6-2 (*Continued*)

Account Code	Category	Adult Services	Information and Programming Services	Circulation Services	Interlibrary Loan	Nonprint Services
500300	Communications					
500301	Postage	7,357	625	5,700	938	94
500302	Telephone	3,660	1,600	1,310	650	100
500303	Datalines	12,806	11,190	623	788	205
600300	Memberships and Conferences					
600301	Dues	750	500	—	—	250
600302	Conference	—	—	—	—	—
700300	Staff Development					
700301	Travel	2,000	1,300	300	200	200
700302	Other	200	130	30	20	20
800300	Contracted Services					
800301	Computer Programming	7,000	5,135	1,210	—	655
800302	Utilities	3,510	1,710	—	1,800	—
900300	Equipment and Repairs					
900301	Minor Equipment	—	—	—	—	—
900302	General Maintenance	250	50	100	50	50
900303	Van Costs	1,000	500	500	—	—
900304	Insurance	750	375	375	—	—
900205	Repairs	500	50	300	75	75
	TOTAL OPERATING	$43,795	24,424	11,923	5,016	2,432
GRAND TOTAL		$711,320	362,823	240,721	48,033	59,743

In constructing their current year's budgets, all service units in the New Age Library followed the adult services model. The summary budget, illustrated in Figure 6-3, brings them all together. The library's current overall goals and objectives, discussed in Chapter 1, precede the summary budget:

Goal 1: The library will serve a larger number of groups now underserved.

Objective 1: Complete a market analysis of the community within four months to identify who is underserved.

Objective 2: Increase the number of active library users by at least 10 percent in the next two years.

Goal 2: In cooperation with local agencies, the library will initiate services that enhance the economic viability of the community.

Objective 1: Contact agencies that work with the major underserved groups (adult as well as youth, identified as at-risk) and develop collaborative plans within the current year to mobilize services for them.

Objective 2: Capture 20 percent more users from at-risk groups over the next three years.

With funding needs in hand for its services, the New Age Library's financial planning team can tally the exact figures under categories common to all library operations and submit them to decision makers in one budget for the entire library. The total request is the sum for all programs.

THE PERFORMANCE FORMAT

Following the model of the program format, the performance format forecast also is built around the library's service units. It uses the goals and objectives and figures of the program approach and adds to them workload performance measures—or service output—and unit costs. It calculates the cost of providing a unit of service by dividing the output totals—in service supplied—into the input costs, or resources allocated in dollars and cents. In other words, it calculates the cost of performance for each service unit.

It is important to create output measures that accurately reflect

---

FIGURE 6-3   Current Year Program Summary Budget

New Age Library

Account Code	Category	Total Budget	Administrative Services	Adult Services	Children's Services	YA Services	Technical Services
100300	**Personnel**						
100301	Full-time	600,765	50,050	310,705	56,000	24,000	160,010
100302	Part-time	117,933	5,200	51,958	21,710	12,000	27,065
100303	Overtime	8,817	—	4,097	4,205	515	—
200300	**Benefits**						
200301	Social Security	55,654	4,227	28,057	6,266	2,793	14,310
200302	Pension	60,959	5,005	31,480	6,021	2,452	16,001
200303	Health Insurance	48,061	4,004	24,856	4,480	1,920	12,802
	TOTAL PERSONNEL	$892,189	68,486	451,153	98,682	43,680	230,188
300300	**Materials**						
300301	Books	188,086	—	119,350	49,730	19,006	—
300302	Periodicals	49,913	—	46,552	2,613	598	150
300303	Databases	23,343	—	19,191	2,500 (jt)		1,652
300304	Documents	5,761	—	5,069	162	320	210
300305	Media	26,210	—	26,210	—	—	—
	TOTAL MATERIALS	$293,313	—	216,372	55,005	19,924	2,012
400300	**Supplies**						
400301	Office	5,618	1,009	2,074	1,110	375	1,050
400302	Computer	3,413	300	1,938	500 (jt)		675

FIGURE 6-3 (*Continued*)

Account Code	Category	Total Budget	Administrative Services	Adult Services	Children's Services	YA Services	Technical Services
				Programs			
500300	Communications						
500301	Postage	13,482	620	7,357	2,170	610	2,725
500302	Telephone	6,815	810	3,660	1,448 (jt)		897
500303	Datalines	14,445	—	12,806	676 (jt)		963
600300	Memberships and Conferences						
600301	Dues	3,000	1,000	750	500 (jt)		750
600302	Conference	1,095	1,095	—	—	—	—
700300	Staff Development						
700301	Travel	5,000	1,000	2,000	1,000 (jt)		1,000
700302	Other	500	—	200	100 (jt)		200
800300	Contracted Services						
800301	Computer Programming	8,250	—	7,000	1,050	200	—
800302	Utilities	10,510	—	3,510	600	250	6,150
900300	Equipment and Repairs						
900301	Minor Equipment	500	500	—	—	—	—
900302	General Maint.	1,250	250	250	250	250	250
900303	Van Costs	2,000	—	1,000	500	500	—
900304	Insurance	1,500	—	750	375	375	—
900205	Repairs	1,000	—	500	250	—	250
	TOTAL OPERATING	$78,378	6,584	43,795	10,529	2,560	14,910
GRAND TOTAL		$1,263,880	75,070	711,320	164,216	66,164	247,110

(jt) = Shared costs between YA and Children's Services.

the key work performed. Consider costing out a bookmobile service by dividing the number of bookmobiles—four—into the total bookmobile costs—$36,000: $36,000/4. Using this approach would mean that it costs $9,000 per bookmobile to provide service—clearly a cost per unit that would be out of line with those of other services. A more important and meaningful statistic would show the number of people served or the number of items circulated—that is, the volume of activity. To help you set workload performance measures that present an effective case for support, review *Output Measures for Public Libraries*.[2]

Figure 6-4 is the New Age Library's current budget presented in a summary performance format. The output totals for each service unit are divided into input costs. For each service unit, the budget line contains the allocated input, the measure of output on the objective, and the unit cost. Figure 6-5, the adult services budget, is broken down into its subprograms. The performance

---

FIGURE 6-4   Current Performance Summary Budget

Program	$	Workload Performance Measures	Unit Costs ($)
Administration	75,070	7,900	9.50
Adult Services	711,320	475,249	1.50
Children's Services	164,216	101,683	1.61
Young Adult Services	66,164	38,507	1.72
Technical Services	247,110	46,133	5.36
TOTAL	$1,268,880	669,472	$1.89

FIGURE 6-5 Current Performance Budget: Adult Services

New Age Library

Subprograms	$	Workload Performance Measures	Unit Costs ($)
Information and Programming Services	362,823	235,840	1.54
Circulation	240,721	195,224	1.23
Interlibrary Loan	48,033	12,075	3.98
Nonprint Services	59,743	32,110	1.86
TOTAL	$711,320	475,249	$1.50

budget takes the basic outline of the program budget and provides more detail by calculating unit costs for the subprograms.

THE ZERO-BASE BUDGET (ZBB) FORMAT

The zero-base budget format combines the goals and objectives of the program format with the service output measures of the performance format and adds to them its own unique feature: a priority ranking of services. This listing builds an element of control over cutbacks by indicating to funding decision makers where cuts will be made if resources are not sufficient to support services as projected. The lowest priority is cut first. This approach helps ensure that no arbitrary reductions will be made.

What sets the ZBB apart from the other three formats is that it requires you to justify your entire budget from scratch. Every year you have to look at each service unit and determine whether or not it should be funded by asking questions like: Should the service be abolished or continued? If the budget increases next year, will the costs outweigh the benefits?

Forecasting using the ZBB is a four-step process:

1. Identify decision units: As you'll see in Figure 6-6, the New Age Library's budget summary using the ZBB contains expenditures for the current fiscal year and forecasts the next fiscal year. The service units used in the program and performance formats—administration, adult, children's, young adult, and technical services—have been retained here as decision units. This format concludes with information added on the current year's actual service output, the predicted output for the forecasted year, and the anticipated change in output and resources required. In other words, the format focuses on and compares expenditures to provide service.

In the ZBB format, the New Age Library can show how it is able to add the Development Office and open the Career Center. Service increases are forecast at 8.8 percent while the money needed to support the service is forecast at only a 5.0 percent increase.

Each decision unit is further broken out into subprograms. For instance, in the current budget, adult services has been divided into reference, readers advisory, and information and referral, as well as circulation, programs, nonprint, and interlibrary loan—stressing service to people. Your library should define its decision units in terms that will present the best case for support. By the end of the planning cycle, forecasts for adult services would not only include the Career Center but also services for older adults, with their respective operating costs broken out.

2. Formulate a decision package: The decision unit's goals and objectives are affirmed. The costs for the activities of each decision unit are calculated so that fiscal decision-makers can compare each one to others competing for money. The services provided by each decision unit are listed along with changes or improvements over current operations. Predicted increases in service are laid out alongside requested increases in support.

Figure 6-7 breaks out the costs to provide adult services and shows the kind of detail you can get from a decision package. You'll see the actual output from the current year, the predicted output for the coming year, the expected change in the output, and the concomitant change in resources needed to accomplish the level of service projected.

FIGURE 6-6 Summary Zero-Base Forecast for FY 1

New Age Library

Decision Units	Workload Performance Measures		F.T.E.		Resources ($)	
	Current	Proposed	Current	Proposed	Current	Proposed
Administration	7,900	8,100	2.5	2.5	75,070	78,138
New Development	—	765	—	.5	—	16,975
Adult Services	475,249	511,290	20.5	20.4	711,320	733,158
New Career Center	—	5,110	—	.5	—	24,642
Children's Services	101,683	111,188	6.6	6.3	164,216	169,701
Young Adult Services	38,507	40,140	2.5	2.5	66,164	70,303
Technical Services	46,133	51,609	11.2	9.5	247,110	233,626
TOTAL	669,472	728,202	43.3	41.7	1,263,880	1,326,543
% CHANGE		8.8%		-3.7%		5.0%

To increase service 8.8 percent requires a 5 percent increase in resources.

FIGURE 6-7   Zero-Base Budget Decision Package Forecasting Adult Services for FY 1

1. PACKAGE NAME: Adult Services

2. SERVICE GOALS AND OBJECTIVES:

1. **Goal**   To provide reference, readers advisory and I&R services, materials and programming for the potential and current adult customers in the community.

   Objective   Provide timely, accurate responses to telephone and walk-in queries via print, nonprint, and electronic sources.

2. **Goal**   To collaborate with other community agencies to implement the Career Center to assist the unemployed and other job seekers.

   Objective   Maintain an up-to-date database of community information and agencies for referral (I&R)

3. CHANGES/IMPROVEMENTS FROM CURRENT OPERATIONS:

Initiate services to community job seekers through a Career Center.

FIGURE 6-7   (*Continued*)

4. Decision Units	Workload Performance Measures		F.T.E.		Resources ($)	
	Current	Proposed	Current	Proposed	Current	Proposed
Reference	164,326	180,698	6	6	239,595	249,178
Readers Advisory	43,333	47,650	3.7	3.5	63,186	63,682
I&R	20,461	22,500	1.5	1.5	29,833	31,026
Programming	7,720	8,200	1.4	1.9	30,213	33,690
Circulation	195,224	205,842	5	4	240,721	241,563
Interlibrary Loan	12,075	12,700	1.5	1.5	48,033	50,169
Nonprint Services	32,110	33,700	1.4	1.5	59,743	63,850
Career Center (NEW)		5,110		.5		24,642
TOTAL	475,249	516,400	20.5	20.4	$711,320	$757,800
5. % CHANGE	8.7%		-.1%		6.5%	

FIGURE 6-8   Decision Package Ranking

RANK	Package Name Adult Services	F.T.E. Current Positions	Proposed Positions	Current Resources	Proposed Resources
1	Circulation	5	4	240,721	241,563
2	Reference	6	6	239,595	249,178
3	Readers Advisory	3.7	3.5	63,186	63,682
4	Programming	1.4	1.9	30,213	33,690
5	Interlibrary Loan	1.5	1.5	48,033	50,169
6	Nonprint Services	1.4	1.5	59,743	63,850
7	I&R	1.5	1.5	29,833	31,026
8	Career Center (NEW)		.5		24,642
	TOTAL	20.5	20.4	$711,320	$757,800
	Change	-.1			6.5%

3. Rank decision packages: An evaluation is made of the costs of decision packages vis-à-vis their contribution to reaching the service objectives of the decision units. The subprograms in each service unit are ranked in priority order.

For instance, in the case of the New Age Library, the managers of reference, readers advisory, programming, circulation, non-print, interlibrary loan, and information and referral each would create a decision package for their subprogram and submit it to the head of adult services. Together, they would rank all subprograms in the adult services decision package. This is a process of negotiation and discussion among the managers of the subprograms. (For more information on the priority-setting process, see *Planning Process for Libraries.*[3]) The final decision is based on the costs of each decision package and each package's importance in the effort to reach the goals and objectives of adult services. Figure 6-8 illustrates how decision packages are ranked.

4. Rank overall: Top managers within the library, and later within the parent organization, merge the priorities of all the decision units they receive into a single priority list of decision packages. At the New Age Library, the managers of the decision units—children's, young adult, adult, and technical services—would meet with the library's top administrators, look over all the decision packages, and negotiate a single priority list for the entire library. Later, the decision makers of the parent organization will rank the library's decision packages with those from all other service agencies within the community. This way, if cuts have to be made, they occur collectively from the bottom up—the last item listed is considered the lowest priority.

CREATING YOUR THREE-YEAR BUDGETARY FORECAST

With the budget format chosen, you are ready to use your current budget to forecast expenditures over the next three years. Before beginning the forecast—no matter the format—you have to:

1. Refer to the financial goals and objectives you set in Chapter 5 to determine their impact on the dollar figures you are going to forecast.

2. Determine other factors that will influence costs (for example, legally binding contractual agreements; salary schedules; and predictable increases in personnel, supplies, materials, and other operating costs).

On Worksheet 6-1 you can list your financial goals and objectives along with other factors that will impact costs.

Worksheet 6-2 supplies you with an outline for constructing your three-year budgetary forecast using the line-item format. The expenditure categories included are general guidelines. Adapt the worksheet to your local situation. For assistance, refer to Figure 6-1, which shows the New Age Library's line-item forecast.

If you are preparing your forecast using the program format, your first task is to identify your service units and the subprograms within each unit. Use Worksheet 6-3 to compose this list. Remember, service units that make the strongest case for funding are built around services to people.

Worksheet 6-4 can be used to create your forecasts for each subprogram, as well as for the summary budget for each of the three years of the financial plan. The horizontal grid will, of course, be determined by your choice of service units and subprograms. For assistance, refer back to Figure 6-2, the New Age Library's adult services forecast, and Figure 6-3, its summary budget.

Forecasting using the performance format means you have to have in place the information comprising the program forecast to which you will add funding input, workload performance measures, and unit costs. Worksheet 6-5 can be used for those calculations. See Figures 6-4 and 6-5 for the New Age Library's summary and adult services forecasts to see how these calculations are used.

Using the zero-base format to forecast, you will begin with the financial goals and objectives from the program forecast and the workload measures from the performance forecast and add decision packages and a priority listing of the packages. Figure 6-6 illustrates the New Age Library's ZBB summary.

With Worksheet 6-6 you can create each decision package for the three years of the financial plan. As with the service units in the program budget, the choice of decision packages should be based on service to people. Refer to Figure 6-7, the New Age Library's adult services decision package, and then record on the worksheet the service goal and objectives; changes or improvements from current operations (a brief statement of a new service, a service enhancement, or deletion of a service); workload performance, where you'll calculate workload measures for each sub-

WORKSHEET 6-1   Factors Affecting the Forecast

List here the financial goals and objectives you set in Chapter 5 that will influence expenditures:

1. _____

_____

2. _____

_____

3. _____

_____

4. _____

_____

5. _____

_____

List here other factors that could influence expenditures, such as a union contract or a predictable increase in the cost of periodicals:

1. _____

_____

2. _____

_____

3. _____

_____

4. _____

_____

5. _____

_____

WORKSHEET 6-2   Line-Item Budget Forecast

Expenditure Categories	Year 1	Year 2	Year 3
Personnel			
Full-time			
Part-time			
Overtime			
Other*			
Benefits			
Social Security			
Pension			
Health Insurance			
Other*			
Total Personnel			
Materials			
Books			
Periodicals			
Databases			
Documents			
Media			
Other*			
Total Materials			
Supplies			
Office			
Computer			
Other*			
Communications			
Postage			
Telephone			
Datalines			
Other*			
Membership and Conferences			
Dues			
Conference			
Other*			
Staff Development			
Travel			
Other*			

*Add here categories specific to your local situation.

WORKSHEET 6-2 (continued)

Expenditure Categories	Year 1	Year 2	Year 3
Contracted Services			
Programming			
Utilities			
Other**			
Equipment and Repairs			
Minor equipment			
General maintenance			
Van costs			
Insurance			
Repairs			
Other**			
Total Operating			
GRAND TOTAL			

*This Worksheet can be used to create forecasts for each subprogram or service unit as well as for summary budgets for each of the three years of the financial plan. Simply modify the horizontal grid to reflect your library's subprograms and service units and label each forecast Year 1, Year 2, or Year 3.

**Add here categories specific to your local situation.

WORKSHEET 6-3 Service Units and Subprograms for Program Budget

List below the service units you have identified for the program budget forecast, and include under each its subprograms:

Service Unit:

   Subprograms:

Service Unit:

   Subprograms:

Service Unit:

   Subprograms:

Service Unit:

   Subprograms:

Service Unit:

   Subprograms:

Service Unit:

   Subprograms:

Service Unit:

   Subprograms:

Service Unit:

   Subprograms:

WORKSHEET 6-4 Program Budget Forecast

YEAR __

Expenditure Categories	Service Unit* or Subprogram
Personnel	
Full-time	
Part-time	
Overtime	
Other**	
Benefits	
Social Security	
Pension	
Health Insurance	
Other**	
Total Personnel	
Materials	
Books	
Periodicals	
Databases	
Documents	
Media	
Other**	
Total Materials	
Supplies	
Office	
Computer	
Other**	
Communications	
Postage	
Telephone	
Datalines	
Other**	

WORKSHEET 6-4 (continued)

Expenditure Categories	Service Unit* or Subprogram
Membership and Conferences	
Dues	
Conferences	
Other**	
Staff Development	
Travel	
Other**	
Contracted Services	
Programming	
Utilities	
Other**	
Equipment and Repairs	
Minor equipment	
General maintenance	
Van costs	
Insurance	
Repairs	
Other**	
Total Operating	
GRAND TOTAL	

*This Worksheet can be used to create forecasts for each subprogram or service unit as well as for summary budgets for each of the three years of the financial plan. Simply modify the horizontal grid to reflect your library's subprograms and service units and label each forecast Year 1, Year 2, or Year 3.

**Add here categories specific to your local situation.

WORKSHEET 6-5 Calculations for Performance Budget Forecast

YEAR:

Subprogram or Service Unit*	Input ($)	Workload Performance Measures	Unit Costs

Note: Unit Cost ($) = $\dfrac{\text{Input}}{\text{Workload measure (units of service supplied)}}$

*This worksheet can be used to calculate unit costs for each service unit and subprogram for the three years of the financial plan. Simply modify the vertical grid to reflect your library's situation and label each worksheet Year 1, Year 2, or Year 3.

WORKSHEET 6-6 Zero-Base Budget Forecast Decision Package

1. Package Name:*

2. Service Goals and Objectives:

3. Changes/Improvement from Current Operations:

4.

Decision Units	Workload Performance Measures		F.T.E.		Resources ($)		5. % Change
	Current	Proposed	Current	Proposed	Current	Proposed	

*This Worksheet can be used to create decision packages for each year of the Financial plan. Simply label each form according to the current year and projected year in items 4 and 5.

WORKSHEET 6-7 Decision Package Ranking

R A N K	Package Name Subprograms	F.T.E. Current Positions	Proposed Positions	Current Resources	Proposed Resources
1					
2					
3					
4					
5					
6					
7					
8					
9					
10					
11					
12					
13					
14					
15					
16					
17					
18					
19					
20					
TOTAL					
Change					

*This worksheet can be used to rank subprograms within each decision package as well as all decision packages into one priority list.

program; and resources required, which will indicate the amount of money needed to supply the volume of service shown in the workload performance. The object, of course, is to raise the workload performance measure as high as possible while keeping costs as low as possible.

Once all decision packages are formulated, you are ready for Worksheet 6-7, where you will rank them. You can use this worksheet to prioritize each decision unit within each decision package for the three years of the planning cycle, as well as to rank all decision packages for the library into one priority list. Look again at Figure 6-8, which shows how the New Age Library ranked its decision packages.

The forecasting and budgeting format you choose depends in part on the political, legal, and financial situation in which your library operates, as well as the cost, time, and level of expertise required to execute it. But in periods of financial distress, when resources are limited and the word cutback is supreme, the ZBB does build funding priorities into the process.

If your library must submit its funding requests to decision makers in a line-item format because of jurisdictional requirements, you can still use ZBB on a regular basis as the library's internal planning document and translate it into line items for outside decision makers. For financial planning, however, we recommend the ZBB. Its forecasts supply the most comprehensive data and allow you to exercise greater control over your expenditures.

ENDNOTES

1. Philip Rosenberg, *Cost Finding for Public Libraries* (Chicago: American Library Association, 1985), 23–55.
2. Nancy VanHouse, Mary Jo Lynch, Charles R. McClure, Douglas L. Zweizig, and Eleanor Jo Roger, *Output Measures for Public Libraries*, 2nd ed. (Chicago: American Library Association, 1987), 35–72.
3. Vernon E. Palmour, Marcia C. Bellassai, and Nancy V. DeWath, *Planning Process for Public Libraries* (Chicago: American Library Association, 1980), 217–227.

7 FUNDING STRATEGIES

Forecasting expenditures over the three-year planning period only gives you half the funding picture. The other half requires an equally in-depth forecast of income to meet these expenditures. You have already considered how you can maximize the use of your library's resources by addressing operating inefficiencies and by stabilizing costs. You have investigated collaborative mobilization of resources with other agencies for cost-effective service provision. And you have made a realistic assessment of the expenditures needed to support the services your library will provide over the life of the financial plan. Now you are going to concentrate on gathering the income necessary to fund those expenditures.

At least two other courses of action can add funds to those you receive or can keep the funds you have from eroding:

1. forecasting and cultivating sources of income
2. developing an investment program.

Using these two strategies, along with those described in earlier chapters, you can go a long way toward making your financial goals and objectives attainable.

STRATEGY
The art of devising or employing plans to reach a goal.

STRATEGY 1

FORECAST AND CULTIVATE SOURCES OF INCOME

In Chapter 2 you gathered data on the library's past and current sources of income by creating a list on Worksheet 2-8, including dollar amounts and percentages of the total income from each. You could call this a "mini" financial history of your income sources.

It's time to analyze those sources—tapped and untapped—a bit further. Worksheet 7-1 brings data forward from Worksheet 2-9. It already shows the sources of income for which you calculated dollar amounts and percentages of total income. Look at the list critically. How well balanced are the amounts? Are you too dependent on one or two sources, and not making the most of others? Have you tried to dig as deeply as possible to get all that you can?

Next, consider those sources you haven't tapped recently—or at all. Identifying sources that are underused or unused will give your library specific direction for future action. Estimate the

WORKSHEET 7-1 Current and Projected Sources of Income   FY___

	Current Sources		Projected Sources	
	$ Realized	% of Total	Projected $	Projected % of Total
Taxation				
Endowment				
Grants				
Federal				
State				
Corporate				
Private Foundation				
Community Foundation				
Other				
Gifts				
Investments				
Bond program				
Contract-for-service				
to libraries				
Annual Campaign				
Direct mail				
Other				
Tributes and memorials				
Membership Programs				
Fees				
Photocopying				
Reserves				
Fees for service				
Other				
Fines				
Overdues				
Other				
Sales				
Buttons				
Bookstore				
Tee shirt				
Other				
Special Events				
Used book sale				
Author reception				
Library anniversary				
Raffle auction				
"Thon"				

amount of dollars you believe can come from the new sources—
or at least a percentage of the total income you hope to achieve
with some hard work—to meet the expenditures you project over
the next three years.

For example, the New Age Library prepared its income forecast
for three years after they projected their expenditures. The income
forecast for the current year had to reach $1,263,880. For Fiscal
Year 1 of the financial plan, it had to reach $1,321,939 just to
clear expenses. Use Worksheet 7-1 to analyze your income and
its sources. Like the New Age Library, your income forecasts must
at least cover your expenditure forecasts.

To help you in your analysis, the following brief descriptions
provide highlights of the 12 income sources listed on the worksheet.

Taxation: Local property taxes contribute at least 80 percent of
most publicly supported libraries' funding. Other sources of tax
revenue are the federal and state governments. Federal agencies—
LSCA for public libraries and HEA Title II for academic libraries—supply this funding. A major portion of HEA is awarded
directly from the U.S. Department of Education; LSCA monies
are received primarily through state library agencies. Funding can
also come from appropriations by state legislatures.

Endowments: Assets contributed by individual donors, outside
agencies, or policy-making bodies, such as the library board of
trustees. Three types of endowments can be established. The *true
endowment* consists of money given in trust; the principle is
invested and only interest earned can be allocated. The *term
endowment* allows the principle to be used, but at a future date,
such as upon the death of the donor. The *quasi-endowment* is
created by the library's governing body from the library's assets.
These assets form the principle of the endowment, but the principle does not have to remain intact. The quasi-endowment allows
the organization to use the assets, based on the discretionary decision of the trustees.

Grants: Awards of money made by a sponsoring agency on a
competitive basis to address a significant need. Grants can be
allotted for seed money, matching funds, service, personnel,
equipment, general operating funds, demonstrations, and model
programs.

The type of grant awarded depends on the granting agency.
Corporations prefer to fund ongoing, successful programs. They

may supply expert personnel to help with the proposal's implementation, as well as equipment and money. The government and foundations are more likely to give seed money or matching funds for start-up to support innovative programs, particularly those seeking to establish a demonstration or model for others. Most libraries apply for grants sponsored by the government—even though both foundations and corporations are also lucrative sources.

QUESTIONS TO ASK ABOUT FUNDING SOURCES

Applying for a grant is a time-consuming process, so it is important to begin by finding out whether your library's request matches the funding profile of the agency you are considering.

Area of support: Does the agency have a history of making awards to libraries or other information, cultural, and educational organizations?

Geography: Does the agency make grants that are local, regional, national, and/or international? Does it fund organizations in a specific locale? your locale?

Type of support: Does the agency provide seed money or matching funds; service, personnel, equipment, and general operating funds; support for demonstrations and model programs?

Demographics: Does the funding agency support services to specific populations?

Investment: The use of money for the purpose of making more money. This is discussed in greater detail later on in this chapter.

Bond program: A type of referendum where the public votes to decide whether to fund big-ticket items, like the purchase or construction of a new library building, or an increase in the percentage of tax revenue apportioned to the library. Since the referendum is a political activity, it should be planned months in advance. It entails learning about your opposition and informing the electorate about why the library is seeking this course of action.

The ideal situation is to have the library on the ballot all by itself. If the ballot is shared with persons running for office, they may see the need to take a stand one way or another on the library issue. Even if you pick a date eight months in advance, you may find that other issues will have been joined to yours for the vote since it costs less to use the ballot for more than one purpose.

The key to referendum success is to involve as many supporters as you can. A referendum will cost money, and since you need money—or you would not be going to the trouble of a referendum in the first place—it is important to find the individuals and organizations that will defray the costs for you. Friends groups usually are prominent in these efforts.

Contract-for-service provided to other libraries: Many libraries that participate in multitype networks supply to other member libraries special services, collections, and technologies, for which they are paid on a contract-for-service basis.

Annual campaign: An appeal to raise funds. This is a controversial approach. Some believe that using an annual campaign to support current operations is risky, that it should be reserved for a specific one-time need. Others find the campaign a dependable way to supplement local funding. The strategy is to collect small cash donations—not property or stock—from many individuals, which are payable immediately.

One type of annual campaign is conducted via direct mail. This approach can be very successful; one-third of all philanthropic giving in the United States is solicited this way. A mail campaign provides direct, intimate contact with the public. Mass mailing is not as successful as writing individualized letters, a task made easier by computers.

Tributes and memorials: A means of honoring someone in a way that keeps their memory alive. Traditionally, plates are placed in books to honor someone who is or was actively involved in the life of the library. The San Diego Public Library has taken this idea one step further. They have solicited contributions of $300 annually in perpetuity, for which they will place a contributor's name in as many books as cost will allow. The library makes it easy to give by allowing payments over four installments and by accepting credit cards.

Gifts: Items voluntarily presented to the library without compensation. The gifts most frequently given are used books, but the Janesville (Wisconsin) Public Library has carried out a much more ambitious gift program. The library created a catalog around its wish list that begins with items costing $25 (such as subscriptions to a periodical) and goes all the way up to $900,000 to fund a mini-branch. In its introductory pages, the catalog contains a statement of what the library needs, why it needs the items listed, and why the residents of the community and its surrounding areas should be interested in helping make the wish list a reality.

Deferred giving is becoming increasingly popular. Potential donors are asked to put the library in their will or to leave the library an annuity or a life insurance policy.

Membership programs: Monies are paid to belong to a group. It can be an Angels Club, in which all members contribute $1,000 or more to the library. It also can be a Friends of the Library group. When the San Antonio Friends Association wanted to increase the number of their members and solicit contributions, the library went to the Public Service Gas and Electric Company and asked them to mail their solicitation letters free-of-charge with residents' utility bills. The result was a highly successful fundraising campaign.

Fees: Still a matter of debate as a source of funding for publicly supported library programs. Most libraries do collect some fees, however, whether for photocopying, lending videocassettes, using online services, or interlibrary loans.

Fines: Libraries bring in some cash by charging for overdue materials, lost books, etc.

Sales: More and more libraries are finding more and more things to sell. Some, like the Birmingham (Alabama) Public Library, have actually opened a retail store on their premises to sell items like books, stationery, art objects, and T-shirts. Others like the Enoch Pratt Free Library in Baltimore operate used book shops, either on a self-service basis or with Friends of the Library. More aggressive entrepreneurial activities include inviting the U.S. Post Office to sell stamps, as the Kansas City Public Library has.

Some libraries are liquidating assets they believe are inappropriate for them to hold. The Kansas City Public Library, for example, successfully sold a valuable painting through Christie's auction house in New York City. Other libraries, however, have found that this practice can unleash political tumult.

The Paterson (New Jersey) Free Public Library, for instance, owned a multimillion dollar art collection, which was housed in a nonpublic area. The library could not afford the cost of keeping it both open to the public and secure. In fact, some of the works got damaged and began to show the effects of lack of climate control. Badly in need of money, the library tried to sell its collection. As soon as word got out, and despite the fact that the work had not been on display and was becoming damaged, the library found itself in the middle of a political squabble about whether it had the right to do so.

Special events: The classic library special event is the used book sale. Other special events include author receptions; the grand opening of a new building, wing, or program; the library's anniversary; a raffle or auction; celebrity sporting events; and the increasingly popular "thon" event (phonathon, readathon, walkathon, etc.).

HOW IS THE DECISION TO GIVE MADE?

Understanding why individuals give and what convinces organizations to fund proposals, and incorporating this knowledge into your campaign to find alternate sources of support, is important for success. While you can assume that money is given by individuals for altruistic reasons, fundraisers say there are many powerful motivators. For some people, it is hard to say no, especially when the one doing the asking is a friend. Others want to belong—to be a member of the Friends group or to have their name placed on a plaque in a prominent place. Many want approval for good deeds or want to share with the less fortunate. Still others are committed to what the library does.

Librarians frequently think that simply uniting a meritorious idea with effective writing skills is all that is needed to win a grant from an organization. But there are five concerns that all proposals must address:

1. *Purpose*: The match between the interests and priorities of the funding agency and the library.
2. *Need*: The extent to which the proposal addresses a significant need.
3. *Accountability*: The degree of success that can be anticipated in the implementation of the proposal, based on the library's prior track record.
4. *Competence*: The level of previous experience and preparation of the personnel assigned to implementation.
5. *Feasibility*: The congruence of the amount of money sought with the job outlined, the suitability of available facilities, and the level of administrative support.

The most frequent cause of failure to win support for a proposal is careless application preparation. This often stems from inadequate attention to details. At the top of the problem list are ignoring instructions and poor clerical preparation. Most grant proposals are ruled out of contention before they are even reviewed for content.

ESTABLISHING A DEVELOPMENT PROGRAM

Today libraries are realizing the advantages of establishing a development program. The New Age Library set financial objectives that resulted in the creation of a program and the appointment of a full-time officer to run it. The development officer became a member of the financial planning team. One of her first tasks was to determine how monies raised would be managed.

Three methods of receiving and managing money are generally followed: 1) the library or parent organization accepts the responsibility; 2) the library's board sets up a foundation or another tax entity on behalf of the library; 3) an existing support group, like the Friends of the Library, takes on the tasks. So that there is no confusion about what to do when the money begins to arrive, it is very important to decide on your approach.

Another task to complete early on is to decide what funding

sources to approach—and in what order—by considering time, cost, and expertise. First, you must consider how soon you need the money. For instance, if you decide to apply for a grant, you have to know agency funding cycles. If a particular agency releases money in December, but you need it in July, your timelines clearly are not compatible.

You also must balance the cost of going after the money with the money you expect to earn. From running a bookstore to designing and carrying out a direct mail campaign, a well-thought-out development plan will cost money. Finally, you must consider if you can handle the effort, even with a development officer, or whether you will need a consultant.

When the New Age Library's development officer looked at the various sources of alternate funding, she penciled several possibilities. The library has held a used book sale annually for a number of years. In the past it has shown a profit, but the development officer also wanted to consider two other possibilities. One was a celebrity auction—a neighboring library had recently conducted one that resulted in a handsome profit. The second was a state library grant of funds to increase service to underserved populations.

To determine if holding their annual book sale before the Christmas holidays would help the library net a profit, the financial planning team did a strategy analysis (see Figure 7-1). They considered the responsibilities for the action steps and dates for initiating and completing each of them. Figure 7-2 shows the estimated expenses, the estimated earnings, and a $500 set-aside, the equivalent of two percent of the total anticipated income, to cover sunk costs—upfront costs they would not be able to recoup if the book sale were not held.

The team did a similar analysis for the other two strategies. Figure 7-3 shows the team's comparison of anticipated expenses, estimated income, and net gain among the three strategies. They discovered that the net gain from the used book sale was the lowest among the three options. The grant application became the first priority, and the celebrity auction moved to second place.

The financial planning team did not forgo the idea of a used book sale, however. They decided that there was an intangible value in holding the sale that could not be met by the other two strategies. It would bring greater visibility to the library and involve a large segment of the community, thereby increasing goodwill.

The process of financial planning reduces risk, but it doesn't totally do away with it. One of the reasons you should do a strategy review is to determine the size of reserve your library needs

FIGURE 7-1   Strategy Analysis, Part 1

Event: Christmas Used-Book Sale

Major Action Step	Person/Group Responsible	Dates of Initiation & Completion	
Facility arrangements	Friends of the Library	Aug. 1	Aug. 30
Inhouse materials selection	Dept. & branch heads	Sept. 10	Dec. 14
Deaccessioning	Technical services staff	"	"
Staffing sale	Friends/staff/volunteers	Dec. 7	"
Publicity	PR staff	Oct. 1	Dec. 21
Coordinating	Co-chairs: Friends & staff	Aug. 1	Dec. 14
Soliciting contributions	Friends & PR staff	all year long	
Transporting materials	Co-chairs & delivery staff	Dec. 5	Dec. 14

FIGURE 7-2   Strategy Analysis, Part 2

Event: Christmas Used-Book Sale

Major Action Step	Anticipated Expense
Facility arrangements	$2,500.00
Inhouse materials selection	2,500.00
Deaccessioning	3,800.00
Staffing sale	1,200.00
Publicity	4,000.00
Coordinating	2,000.00
Soliciting contributions	—
Transporting materials	500.00
TOTAL EXPENSE	$16,500.00

FIGURE 7-3   Strategy Analysis, Part 3

Strategy	Anticipated Expense	Estimated Income	Reserve (.02 x $ Income)	Net Gain
Used-book sale	$16,500.00	$25,000.00	$500.00	$ 8,000.00
Celebrity auction	5,000.00	15,000.00	300.00	9,700.00
Grant application	2,000.00	25,000.00	500.00	22,500.00

WORKSHEET 7-2 Strategy Analysis, Part 1   Event:

Major Action Step	Person/Group Responsible	Dates of Initiation & Completion

WORKSHEET 7-3 Strategy Analysis, Part 2   Event:

Major Action Step	Anticipated Expense

Estimated income: _____
Reserve % (.02): _____
Reserve total: _____

WORKSHEET 7-4   Strategy Analysis, Part 3   Comparative Event Analysis

Strategy	Anticipated Expense	Estimated Income	Reserve (.02 x $ Income)	Net Gain*

*Net gain = Estimated income – Reserves

to meet those risks. In the for-profit business sector, a reserve of money is usually budgeted for unexpected, sometimes catastrophic events—from having an office roof cave in to losing an important client.

Although few libraries do this at present—some are not allowed by their parent organizations—your financial planning team should plan for risk. Library managers must consider resource shortages, overestimating the market, incurring higher costs than estimated, and other potential problems. All of these can affect the library's ability to deliver its programs and services. In order to protect your library from risk, you would do well to maintain a reserve fund of two to three percent of the bottom line. To make money from money on hand, the best place for the reserve fund is in the library's investment program.

Complete your strategy analysis using Worksheets 7-2, 7-3, and 7-4. Worksheet 7-4 has a column that projects reserves based on estimated income. Net gain is the sum left after the reserves are set aside.

Remember, there are tangible as well as intangible results you can gain from many strategies. Weigh them carefully.

STRATEGY 2

DEVELOP AN INVESTMENT PROGRAM

Any sum of money on hand that will not be spent immediately is a candidate for investment. One of the most important facets of your financial plan is not to allow money to lie idle, but rather to plan its use to make more.

INVESTMENT PLANNING

This introduction to investing is in no way a substitute for the knowledge and advice of an expert financial planner. The intention is to show how investing resources fits into your overall financial plan. Also, you must know the state laws under which your library operates, because there are great variations in what is considered a legal investment for a public entity. Some states have no restrictions; others impose severe restrictions.

Give careful thought to what you want the library's money to do. Keeping your financial goals and objectives in mind, ask these five questions:

1. For what purpose do we want to consider investing?
2. Where will we get the money to invest?
3. What types of investment are best for our library?
4. How soon will the library need the money?
5. What are the risks involved?

Of these questions, *why* you are investing the money and the *risks* involved are of the greatest importance.

WHY INVEST? WHAT ARE THE RISKS?

There are at least three reasons to invest: 1) for capital appreciation; 2) for long-term growth; 3) for short-term interest or profit. As you consider how much you want or need to earn, you also should think about risk. What is your library willing or able to risk for the anticipated outcome? How you answer these questions will influence the type of investment vehicles you finally choose.

The key to successful investing is *sensible* risk-taking. That means, simply, understanding the risk involved in each of the financial instruments available. For example, investing only in high-growth stocks is a high-risk strategy. A conservative investment strategy is one in which funds are placed in money markets, blue chip stocks, and municipal bonds. Then there is the diversified strategy. Here a certain percentage of money is invested in both high-growth stocks and low-risk instruments.

Let's briefly review a number of investment vehicles. Your library may already have money invested in one or more of these. If so, and especially if the decision to invest was made some time ago, you should make sure your library is earning all that it can from its money. If your library has put its money in nothing more than an interest-bearing checking account, you have a lot of research to do. This is just the starting point.

Certificates of deposit: Issued by banks, CDs are receipts for funds deposited in banks for a predetermined period of time on which the banks have agreed to a specific rate of interest. At maturity, the CD gives the investor both principal and interest. Maturity dates range from one to eighteen months, but most mature in four months.

Government bonds: Offered by the U.S. Department of the Treasury, bonds generally have the longest maturities, from seven to twenty-five years. Issued in denominations as low as $1,000, bonds have fixed rates of interest and fixed maturity dates.

QUESTIONS TO ASK INVESTMENT AND FINANCIAL ADVISORS

1. Do you have experience working with libraries?
2. Are you a certified advisor? By whom?
3. What is the earning record of your customers—short- and long-term?
4. What is your overriding investment outlook?
5. Do you charge by flat fee? Percentage of assets managed? By the hour? By commission?
6. How much time will you spend on our account? Who will our main contact be?
7. Will you coordinate your work with other professionals we hire, such as our attorney and accountant?
8. How will you keep us informed about our progress? What kinds of reports can we expect to receive?

Government securities: Created by the federal government to finance projects and programs, government securities are backed by the word of the government and are considered very safe investments. As a conservative investment vehicle, they offer competitive yields and are not subject to state or local taxes. The three types of government securities are treasury bills, treasury notes, and U.S. government bonds.

Money markets: A money market is composed of several individual markets, one for each of its short-term credit instruments: treasury bills, commercial paper, certificates of deposit, and bankers' acceptances. The money market is a liquid market offering a high degree of safety of principal because issuers generally have high credit ratings. Money market maturities are short—at least within one year, but most within ninety days or less—so there is low risk of loss as a result of interest rate changes.

Mutual funds: An investment company, organized by an advisory firm, offers mutual fund shareholders specific investment objectives. Mutual funds come under such headings as aggressive growth, growth, growth and income, international, global, precious metals/gold, balanced, income, option/income, corporate bond, U.S. government income, Ginnie Mae, long-term municipal bond, short-term municipal bond, single-state municipal bond, and money market.

A shareholder is part owner of a mutual fund and with other shareholders has the authority to change investment advisors if the fund underperforms. The Securities and Exchange Commission regulates all mutual funds.

Stocks: Stocks represent money or capital made available for investment by corporations in order to fund their enterprise. Investors who buy shares of stocks become part-owners of the corporation. Of course, they are most interested in obtaining return on investment that justifies the risk they took in purchasing the share of stock. Stock prices are influenced by a company's earnings outlook, dividend prospects, and general financial condition—and how investors are interpreting these factors.

Treasury bills: Known as T-bills, these comprise the bulk of government financials. They are sold by the U.S. Department of the Treasury at weekly and monthly auctions in five denominations from $10,000 to $1,000,000. They have maturities from three months to one year. The return to the investor is the dif-

WORKSHEET 7-5   Investment Profile

	Purpose for Investment	Acceptable Level of Risk
Certificates of deposit		
Government bonds		
Government securities		
Money market		
Mutual fund		
Stocks		
Treasury bills		
Treasury notes		
Other		

ference between the purchase price and the face value of the bill at the time of maturity.

Treasury notes: Usually issued by the U.S. Department of the Treasury in $1,000 denominations, notes have maturities between one and seven years, so they often offer higher yields than T-bills. Notes have a fixed rate of interest which is paid semiannually.

WHAT SHOULD YOU INVEST IN?

How do you decide what type of financial instrument to invest in? Read books, read the business page of your daily newspaper, talk to people, then hire an expert! There are three types of financial advisors: brokers, who make a commission on any transaction that takes place, whether you make or lose money; advisors, whose fees consist of a percentage of assets managed; and planners, who will work for an agreed-upon fee or commission. You can locate any of these professionals by talking with colleagues, asking your bank for a reference, or using someone already advising your parent organization.

Advance preparation will help the decision-making process go more smoothly. Use Worksheet 7-5 to begin the formulation of your investment profile with your financial advisor. For each of the investment vehicles listed—of course, you can always add to the list—consider why you want to use it and the level of risk acceptable to your library.

PART FOUR

STAYING ON COURSE

8 EVALUATING THE FINANCIAL PLAN

The next step of the financial plan is to resolve how you will assess its success. The plan has to communicate to financial decision makers what key indicators you are going to monitor to determine the plan's performance—to determine whether the library has achieved the desired outcomes.

The evaluation model presented here entails choosing key indicators from the financial data and instruments you have been working with—the fiscal status review, situation and market analyses, financial goals and objectives, budgetary forecasts, and income forecasts and sources—then evaluating the library's progress. For each indicator you will:

1. Acknowledge desired performance
2. Determine actual performance
3. Compare actual and desired performance
4. Identify any deviation
5. Analyze the cause of deviations
6. Set a program of corrective action
7. Implement corrections

These seven steps (see Figure 8-1) comprise a deviation model for evaluating your financial plan. Using it will enable you to measure the improvements you have made in increasing your control over your finances, or to set a course of corrective action if you haven't. The deviations you identify may be beneficial or detrimental to the library's operations. If they are beneficial, you will want to find a way to make them a part of the plan. If they are detrimental, you will want to ensure that they don't happen again.

Some of the most meaningful indicators to review in preparing the evaluation are discussed below. You'll conduct an evaluation at the end of the first year of the financial plan and at the end of each succeeding year.

FINANCIAL STATUS REVIEW

You will begin here as you began in Chapter 2, with the balance sheet. On Worksheet 2-1 you created a current balance sheet. Now, a year later, you can create a second balance sheet on Worksheet 8-1, recording assets, liabilities, and the fund balance. And it is these three numbers that you want to evaluate. Does this year's new balance sheet show changes you desired over the year?

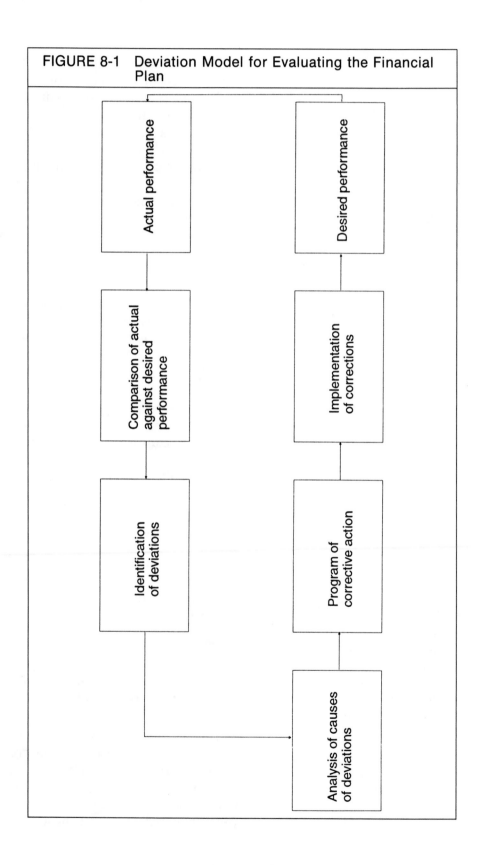

FIGURE 8-1   Deviation Model for Evaluating the Financial Plan

WORKSHEET 8-1 Balance Sheet

	CURRENT FUNDS		BUILDING EQUIPMENT FUND	ENDOWMENT FUND	TOTAL
	Unrestricted	Restricted			
ASSETS					
Current Assets:					
Cash					
Short-term securities					
Fines and fees receivable					
Grants receivable					
Supplies					
Total Current Assets					
Investments					
Land, buildings, and equipment					
Total Assets					
LIABILITIES AND FUND BALANCES					
Current Liabilities:					
Accounts payable					
Accrued expenses					
Current mortgage payment					
Total Current Liabilities					
Total Mortgage Payable					
Total Liabilities					
Fund balances:					
Unrestricted					
Restricted:					
Literacy					
Programming					
Purchase of fixed assets					
Invested in fixed assets					
Endowment funds					
Total Fund Balance					
Total Liabilities and Fund Balances					

WORKSHEET 8-2 Performance of Key Indicators

	Desired Performance	Actual Performance	Comparison	Deviation	Cause	Correction
Assets						
Liabilities						
Fund Balance						
Income						
Expenditures						
Efficiency						
Potential Customers						
New Library Services						
New Channels of Distribution						
New Promotions						
Goals (list)						
Objectives (list)						
Sources of Income (list)						
Investments (list)						

WORKSHEET 8-3   Timeline for Implementation of Corrections

	Activity Undertaken			Staff Assignment	Time Allocation in Days	
	Correction	Begin date	End date		By staff member	Total
Assets						
Liabilities						
Fund Balance						
Income						
Expenditures						
Efficiency						
Potential Customers						
New Library Services						
New Channels of Distribution						
New Promotions						
Goals (list)						
Objectives (list)						
Sources of Income (list)						
Investments (list)						

WORKSHEET 8-4 Evaluate Growth and/or Decline in Library Income

To determine the direction of income trends, add current data to calculations from Worksheet 2-4

Total Library Income	Trends (% +/−)
Current Year	
Fiscal Year 1 (1 year ago)	
Fiscal Year 2 (2 years ago)	
Fiscal Year 3 (3 years ago)	

To complete this worksheet, fill in four years of your library's total income.
To determine growth or decline, use the following formula:

$$\frac{\text{Present year} - \text{Past year}}{\text{Past year}} = \text{Trend}$$

WORKSHEET 8-5   Evaluate Growth and/or Decline in Library Expenditures

To determine the direction of expenditure trends, add current data to calculations from Worksheet 2-5.

	Total Library Expenditures	Trends (% +/–)
Current Year		
Fiscal Year 1 (1 year ago)		
Fiscal Year 2 (2 years ago)		
Fiscal Year 3 (3 years ago)		

To complete this worksheet, fill in four years of your library's total expenditures.
To determine growth or decline, use the following formula:

$$\frac{\text{Present year} - \text{Past year}}{\text{Past year}} = \text{Trend}$$

In general, the desired performance would be an increase in assets and the fund balance and a decrease in liabilities. It also is possible, however, that the balance sheet will show a decrease in assets—if you divested a library asset. Record the desired performance, actual performance, and the corrections you may have to make on Worksheet 8-2 and how you will implement the corrections on Worksheet 8-3. These two worksheets can serve as templates on which you can collect data for the evaluation. Each template can be duplicated to analyze each of the indicators listed and individualized to reflect your particular situation.

In your financial review, you also looked for trends in library income and expenditures by comparing those numbers over the past three years on Worksheets 2-4 and 2-5. Now using Worksheets 8-4 and 8-5, you can compare the current year's income and expenditures with the last three years' figures, then uncover changes in performance and set corrective action on Worksheets 8-2 and 8-3.

SITUATION ANALYSIS

In the situation analysis (Chapter 3) you identified those external and internal conditions affecting the library's ability to deliver its programs and services. On Worksheets 3-1 through 3-6 you recorded information about external conditions: economic indicators, the legal environment, social conditions, technological outlook, organizational restructuring, and political factors. Has anything happened over the past year that is different from what you expected? Record on Worksheet 8-6 any unexpected changes that will influence your library's fiscal performance over the life of the financial plan.

Your examination of internal conditions focused on your library's efficiency in an attempt to increase service while holding the line on cost—or to maintain service if your funding sources are eroding. Other factors, of course, impact on internal conditions—and therefore on operating costs. You were also asked to consider the physical plant, union contract provisions, and work force stability and adequacy. On Worksheet 3-7, you were asked how efficiently your library performs and if there were areas in which you felt improvements could be made.

One year later, has the library assessed its efficiency and implemented improvements? Describe the new situation in your library on Worksheets 8-2 and 8-3.

WORKSHEET 8-6   Review of External Conditions

Describe any unexpected external changes that may have occurred over the past year. How will they influence your library's future financial performance? What will you do to respond to them?

	Change	Influence	Response
1. Economic Indicators			
2. Legal Environment			
3. Social Conditions			
4. Technological Outlook			
5. Organizational Restructuring			
6. Political Factors			

WORKSHEET 8-7   Budgetary Forecasts

Forecast expenditures for the next two years using the budget format selected in Chapter 6.

MARKET ANALYSIS

The cornerstone of the market analysis (Chapter 4) was the determination of how responsive your library is to its customers. You completed a Community Profile and a Library Profile to measure your current responsiveness. Then you were asked to look into the future and on Worksheets 4-13 through 4-16, you identified four new directions your library could take to attract potential customers through new services, channels of distribution, and library promotions. How have you done? Use Worksheets 8-2 and 8-3 to highlight your successes and pinpoint deviations.

FINANCIAL GOALS AND OBJECTIVES

The success you enjoy in meeting your financial goals and objectives provides the major measure of the success of your library's financial plan. Take a look at the goals and objectives on Worksheet 5-3 that were meant to be accomplished within the first year of your financial plan. Use Worksheets 8-2 and 8-3 to determine if actual performance has met desired performance.

BUDGETARY FORECASTS

Your success in meeting your financial goals and objectives will also influence whether any adjustments have to be made to your three-year budgetary forecast. Was the forecast on target? Returning to your budget format of choice, you can reforecast expenditures for the next two years on Worksheet 8-7.

FUNDING STRATEGIES

It all does finally come down to money. To fund your goals and objectives, to breathe life into your budgetary forecasts—to get from year one to year three of your financial plan and ensure that your library is in better shape than it was before—you need money. In Chapter 7 you determined the income needed to finance the services you projected, and you considered two funding strategies: cultivating new sources of funding and developing an investment program. On Worksheet 7-1 you projected the income your library will require over the three years of the financial plan; on Worksheet 7-2 you analyzed the sources of income being used by the library and those still untapped. You projected the dollars you believed you could obtain from each source. On Worksheet 8-2, indicate which of these sources (including investments) you have investigated and whether you achieved the amount projected. What was the deviation? On Worksheet 8-3, work out how you will implement corrections.

MAKING EVALUATION A PART OF THE FINANCIAL PLAN

Since the evaluation is used to pinpoint necessary improvements, it is an integral part of the financial plan. Its usefulness will go unrealized, however, if no one pays attention to its results. You don't want to come to the end of a fiscal year with results *you* feel are significant and find that there is disagreement among the financial planning team itself or on the part of funding decision-makers on whether *what* you measured tells the complete and accurate story.

Making the evaluation a part of the financial plan is a two-step process. First, your financial planning team has to get feedback from the team members who are external stakeholders. Although they have been involved in the planning process all along, their input at this particular point is invaluable. Since they represent the community at large, they may be able to anticipate possible disagreement with the indicators and recommend adjustments before the plan is submitted to funding decision-makers.

It is, of course, crucial that funding decision-makers agree on the team's choice of indicators—the second step in integrating the evaluation. This occurs when you submit the three-year financial plan to them. At this point, it will only include the outline of the evaluation and the indicators you have set as markers for the plan's success. In fact, the evaluation will look somewhat like the charts in the first part of this chapter, spelling out the kinds of data you will be collecting in Fiscal Years 1, 2, and 3. Receiving the funders' "OK" means they feel the plan is worth funding. In the subsequent three years, the funders will use the comparative data gathered and processed as a result of the evaluation to determine further—or reduced—funding levels.

9 WRAPPING IT UP

The final details of your financial planning effort now command center stage. First, you have to write the Executive Summary—the first pages of the financial plan. Then with the completed financial plan in hand, you will communicate its results as broadly as possible.

THE EXECUTIVE SUMMARY

The Executive Summary is not just an introduction to the financial plan. It is a succinct and factual summary of the details found within the plan itself. Its goal is to capture the readers' interest and gain an early commitment to action—particularly from those who hold the purse strings, like your board, administration, city council, and outside funders like foundation executives and government grant officials.

Although placed at the beginning of the financial plan, the Summary is not written until the entire plan is complete. Some advocate writing the summary first, but too frequently that can result in missed points or vagueness—or cause the writer to try and fit the plan to assumptions presented in the summary. While writing the Executive Summary, keep foremost in mind that one of the main reasons you have prepared the financial plan is to obtain ample funding for the library so that you can provide responsive services to your community.

The format of the Summary should follow the shape of the financial plan. (See the New Age Library's Executive Summary on pages 176–178.) After writing a brief introduction that describes the current status of the library and the community it serves, provide highlights of all the plan's phases: financial status review, situation analysis, market analysis, financial goals and objectives, expenditure and income forecasts, and how you will evaluate the success of the effort.

Conclude the Executive Summary with a short commentary on your expectations for the library's ongoing efforts to serve its constituents successfully. This is the place where you can be less businesslike, where you and your team can radiate vision and energy.

COMMUNICATING RESULTS OF FINANCIAL PLANNING

Once your financial plan is complete, it's time to turn your attention to its dissemination to the community at large, and to its approval by the Board of Trustees (or the policymakers relevant to your particular library environment) and funding decision-makers. This process follows the pattern of an annual event with which you are already familiar—getting the budget passed. Keep in mind, however, that you are not asking for a three-year commitment to the plan. (It is legally impossible for decision makers to bind funds for more than one year.) What you are looking for is agreement that the plan's contents represent a goal you all will work toward.

The importance of having kept policymakers and funding decision makers aware of and involved in the activities of the financial planning team right from the start of the process will now become clear. Although you shouldn't expect the plan to be approved exactly as it is written, it's doubtful that many changes will be requested—unless of course an unforeseen event like a shortfall in taxes occurs. Try to make it clear, however, that you are ready to negotiate any aspect of the plan and revise it if appropriate in order to make going ahead possible.

The approval process may not take place behind closed doors. Because of the Sunshine laws, all discussion concerning the plan must occur in the open. Public hearings must be held and all must be welcome to attend. It is therefore imperative that the presentations and documentation provide a clear picture of the programs currently carried out by the library, those projected for the future, and the funding required to support them. The presentation should be designed so that it can be understood by a wide variety of people—legislators, administrators, financial experts, community officials, citizens, and reporters. The key is simplicity, without omitting important data.

You and your financial planning team will take a back seat during the presentation—now it's time for the board or senior administrators to take over. This doesn't mean your input isn't important at this point. Your role is to prepare your representatives so that they can present your case for support effectively. Their presentation should begin with a review of the Executive Summary, highlighting important findings uncovered in the financial status review, situation and market analyses, financial goals and objectives, and strategies for new sources of funding. It's crucial that they convey what the library faces over the long haul and how it is preparing to deal with it. Finally, the presentation must be concise so that it holds the audience's interest and conveys the facts necessary for approval.

A public library will need a large number of copies of the plan in order to make it available at all hearings and to disseminate to newspapers, civic organizations, and interested citizens. Of course, copies also should be available for inspection in the library.

It is also important to communicate your efforts well beyond the local community—with your colleagues at professional meetings and through the library press. Since the library profession has relatively little acquaintance with formal, systematic financial planning, news of your efforts will help other library managers to at least begin thinking about their libraries' fiscal futures and perhaps convince them that the financial planning process can play an important role.

PREPARING FOR A SOUND FINANCIAL FUTURE

Library managers are operating in what has been referred to as a zero-sum society. Increased financial support for one organization or service requires a reduction in support for another so that the sum total of gains and losses is zero. Decisions on resource allocation are made in a political environment, where those who chart the funding pluses and minuses are more inclined to rely on systematically obtained evidence—hard data—than on simple assertion, intuition, or past practice. This economic fact of life requires aggressive financial planning on the part of libraries. Good intentions can no longer be substituted for good planning.

If your library is to thrive in this competitive arena, it is incumbent on your financial planning team to portray to funding decision-makers the relationship between the services you provide to your community and the resources you are allocated. When you complete the financial planning process in this book, you will be in a strong position to do this—and you will be an advocate in better library management through financial planning.

THE NEW AGE LIBRARY
EXECUTIVE SUMMARY

Hard times have come to the New Age Library, and like other community agencies, it is feeling the economic pinch. Despite this, we feel it is imperative that the library move ahead in developing new services responsive to our current and potential customers.

The three-year financial plan that follows was prepared by a financial planning team consisting of community leaders, funding decision-makers, library managers, library staff, and representatives of the state library. Using surveys, individual focus group interviews, statistics, performance measures, and other documents of record, the team has compiled data on which to build a detailed case for support. The plan:

- Details the library's current fiscal status
- Analyzes the global and local conditions under which the library operates
- Assesses the library's effectiveness in serving its constituents
- Sets financial goals and objectives for the next three years
- Determines the expenditures necessary to meet those goals and objectives
- Projects the library's budget over the next three years
- Presents strategies to diversify sources of income
- Demonstrates how to evaluate the success of the plan.

CURRENT FISCAL STATUS
An analysis of trends over the past three years has demonstrated that the library's expenses have grown disproportionately to income, which is increasingly flat. Taxation remains the major means of support; few sources have been sought outside that annual allocation.

SITUATION ANALYSIS
In documenting the impact of external factors on the library, the financial planning team has found that the local economic downturn is mirroring the broader, national picture. Internally, a series of productivity studies have pinpointed low levels of efficiency in several areas and revealed how funds can be redistributed to improve service while holding the line on costs.

MARKET ANALYSIS
The market analysis has uncovered three growing audiences: the unemployed, latchkey children, and older adults. The community is experiencing shifts in its population. The ranks of the unemployed are rising, particularly among white-collar workers. As the

number of families in which both parents work continues to grow, children with no one at home seek haven in the library until the end of the business day. The proportion of older adult residents is the fastest growing of all age groups—and all indications are that it will continue to spiral well past the year 2000.

As a result of the market analysis, the financial planning team has recommended initiating new services for each of the three audiences: a Career Center to provide information and referral programs to assist job seekers and intergenerational programs to respond to the needs of both children and older adults. The team has also identified developing collaborative services with other agencies as a cost-effective way to initiate the new services.

GOALS AND OBJECTIVES FOR THE FUTURE

More and more residents are visiting the library annually, a sign that they consider the library an important contributor to the community's well-being. Our vision for the next decade is to capitalize on the historically proved significance of the public library. We want to assist the unemployed preparing for new careers, parents looking for assistance in raising their families, and older adults seeking to participate in community life.

The library is convinced of the need to initiate new services despite the prevailing economic conditions. It has set the following financial goals and objectives for the next three fiscal years:

Goal One: To protect the library from future loss of revenue.
   Objective 1: Retain at least two percent of the local government's total appropriation for community services over the next three years.
   Objective 2: Within six months, appoint a development officer who will begin to analyze sources of income and prepare a scheduled plan to diversify.

Goal Two: To maximize the use of library resources.
   Objective 1: Within one year, reduce costs for continuing services at least two percent by addressing inefficiencies uncovered in productivity studies.
   Objective 2: Review operations to stabilize or reduce costs another one percent within two years.

Goal Three: To provide for the library's continued financial growth.
   Objective 1: Over the next two years, to realize further internal savings of two percent, reorganize library service delivery by joining forces with other service agencies to deliver library services to newly discovered audiences.
   Objective 2: Over the next three years add at least five percent each year to the library's total income from new funding sources.

PROJECTING THE BUDGET OVER THREE FISCAL YEARS

Because of the community's high unemployment rate, and since the regional employment agency has agreed to share the start up and ongoing costs of a Career Center, the financial planning team has slated the initiation of that service for FY1, along with the creation of a Development Office. In FY2, services to latchkey children will be added. And in FY3, older adult services will receive the focus of attention.

Using the zero-base budget format, over the next three years projected increases in service remain more than three percent higher than increases in costs.

STRATEGIES TO GATHER THE FUNDING NEEDED

The New Age Library will meet its income goals to increase the amount of outside funding at least five percent per year over the next three fiscal years by aggressively seeking grants, improving our investment program, and undertaking a series of special events.

MEASURING SUCCESS

Measuring the success of the financial plan will demonstrate whether the library is making the right financial moves and where the plan might need modification. Key indicators have been set to monitor how well the library's financial plan helps to achieve the outcomes desired. Using a deviation model, we will: measure the congruence between the library's desired and actual financial performance, identify deviations from the course set, analyze the cause of the deviation, set a program of corrective action, implement the corrections, and iterate the cycle annually.

Indicators that will be monitored include: trends in income and expenditures, improvements in operating efficiency, increases in market penetration, progress made toward reaching goals and objectives, ability to meet budget forecasts, and the ability to raise the income needed to finance the services projected. The past record will be compared with the present plan for the future.

PREPARING FOR A SOUND FISCAL FUTURE

The New Age Library's financial planning team has created a plan that we believe will lead to a sound fiscal future. We have demonstrated the relationship between the magnitude of responsive services the library provides to the community with the level of funding it receives. In this zero-sum society where increased support for one service demands reduction in support for another, library stakeholders realize the importance of planning to maintain control over the library's resources, regardless of economic fluctuations. We believe this three-year plan will do just that and commend it to your attention.

SOURCES

These works were particularly helpful to us as we prepared this book.

CHAPTER 1, FINANCIAL PLANNING AS STRATEGIC PLANNING

Brooks, Julie K. and Barry A. Stevens. *How to Write a Business Plan.* New York: AMACOM Books, 1987.

Connors, Tracy D. and Christopher T. Callaghan. *Financial Management for Nonprofit Organizations.* New York: AMACOM Books, 1982.

Fine, Sara. "Change and Resistance: The Cost/Benefit Factor." *The Bottom Line 5,* 1 (Spring 1991): 18–24.

Gumpert, David E. *How to Write a Successful Business Plan.* Boston: Inc. Publishing, 1990.

Kosekoff, Jacqueline and Arlene Fink. *Evaluation Basics.* Beverly Hills: Sage Publications, 1982.

Martin, Murray, Editor. *Financial Planning for Libraries.* New York: Haworth Press, 1982.

McClure, Charles R., Amy Owen, Douglas L. Zweizig, Mary Jo Lynch, and Nancy A. VanHouse. *Planning and Role Setting for Public Libraries.* Chicago: American Library Association, 1987.

Palmour, Vernon E., Marcia C. Bellassai, and Nancy V. DeWath. *A Planning Process for Public Libraries.* Chicago: American Library Association, 1980.

Penniman, W. David. "On Their Terms: Preparing Libraries for a Competitive Environment," *The Bottom Line 1,* 3 (1987): 11–15.

Prentice, Ann E. *Financial Planning for Libraries.* Metuchen, New Jersey: Scarecrow Press, 1983.

Riggs, Donald. *Strategic Planning for Library Managers.* Phoenix: Oryx Press, 1984.

Rossi, Peter H. and Howard E. Freeman. *Evaluation: A Systematic Approach,* 3rd ed., Beverly Hills: Sage, 1985.

Turock, Betty J. and Andrea Pedolsky. "Financial Planning for a Stable Fiscal Future," *The Bottom Line 5,* 3 (Fall 1991): 13–17.

CHAPTER 2, CURRENT FINANCIAL STATUS

Berger, Sharon, "The First Audit," *The Bottom Line* 5, 2 (Summer 1991): 28–30.

Clark, Philip. "Accounting is Evaluating," *Drexel Library Quarterly* (Summer 1985): 61–74.

Hayes, Sherman and Clifford D. Brown. "Fund Accounting Basics," *The Bottom Line* 3, 3 (1989): 32–33.

Hayes, Sherman and David R. L. Gabhart. "There's Depreciation in Your Future," *The Bottom Line* 2, 2 (1988): 27–28.

Hayes, Sherman and William P. Wiggins. "Should There Be a CPA in Your Life," *The Bottom Line* 2, 4 (1989): 31–32.

Hoogcarspel, Annelies. "Financial Reporting through the Audit," *The Bottom Line* 5, 1 (Spring 1991): 30–32.

Smith, G. Stevenson. *Managerial Accounting for Libraries and other Non-Profit Organizations.* Chicago: American Library Association, 1991.

Spurga, Ronald C. *Balance Sheet Basics: Financial Management for Nonfinancial Managers.* New York: Franklin Watts, 1986.

Steinberg, Erica. "The Balance Sheet: How to Read It and How to Use It," *The Bottom Line* 2, 1 (1988): 20–22.

Tracy, John A. *How to Read a Financial Report,* 2nd ed. New York: John Wiley, 1983.

Wacht, Richard F. *Financial Management in Nonprofit Organizations,* 2nd ed. Atlanta: Georgia State University Business Press, 1991.

CHAPTER 3, THE SITUATION ANALYSIS

Christopher, William F. *Productivity Measurement Handbook.* Cambridge, Massachusetts: Productivity Press, 1985.

Dougherty, Richard M. and Fred J. Heinritz. *Scientific Management of Library Operations,* 2nd ed. Metuchen: Scarecrow Press, 1982.

Goetz, Malcolm. "Libraries and the Business Cycle," *The Bottom Line* 2, 1 (1987): 4–5.

Holzer, Marc, Editor. *Productivity in Public Organizations.* Port Washington: Kennikat Press, 1976.

Reilly, Catherine, "Productivity Measurement for Fiscal Control," *The Bottom Line* Charter Issue (1986): 21–28.

Roberts, S. A. *Cost Management for Library and Information Services.* London: Butterworth, 1985.

Rosenberg, Philip. *Cost Finding for Public Libraries.* Chicago: American Library Association, 1985.

Senkevitch, Judith Jamison. "Analyzing Productivity in the Era of Accountability," *The Bottom Line 5,* 3 (Fall 1991): 25–32.

Tippett, Paul. *Strategies for Productivity,* New York: UNIPUB, 1984.

CHAPTER 4, THE MARKET ANALYSIS

Guerena, Salvador, Editor. *Latino Librarianship.* Jefferson, North Carolina: McFarland and Company, Inc., 1990.

Gumpert, David E. *How to Create a Successful Business Plan.* Boston: Inc. Publishing, 1990.

Heim, Kathleen M. and Danny P. Wallace, Editors. *Adult Services: An Enduring Focus for Public Libraries.* Chicago: American Library Association, 1990.

Kotler, Philip. *Marketing for Nonprofit Organizations,* 2nd ed. New York, Prentice-Hall, 1982.

Lively, Sandra. "Marketing: Can It Improve Cost Effectiveness," *The Bottom Line 4,* 3 (Fall 1990): 12–16.

McClure, Charles R., Amy Owen, Douglas L. Zweizig, Mary Jo Lynch, and Nancy A. VanHouse. *Planning and Role Setting for Public Libraries.* Chicago: American Library Association, 1987.

Stewart, David W. *Focus Groups: Theory and Practice.* Newbury Park, California: Sage Publications, 1990.

Turock, Betty J., Ed. *Evaluating Federally Funded Public Library Programs.* Washington: United States Department of Education, Office of Educational Research and Improvement, Library Programs, 1990.

Turock, Betty J. *Improving Public Library Program Evaluation.* Washington: United States Department of Education, Office of Educational Research and Improvement, Library Programs, 1992.

VanHouse, Nancy, Mary Jo Lynch, Charles R. McClure, Douglas L. Zweizig, and Eleanor Jo Rodger. *Output Measures for Public Libraries,* 2nd ed. Chicago: American Library Association, 1987.

Zweizig, Douglas L., Debra Wilcox Johnson, and Jane B. Robbins. *Evaluation of Adult Literacy Programs.* Chicago: American Library Association, 1990.

CHAPTER 5, ASSUMPTIONS, GOALS, AND OBJECTIVES

Clegg, Charles C. *Goal Setting: The Key to Good Management.* Champaign: Management Learning Laboratories, 1984.

McClure, Charles R., Amy L. Owen, Douglas L. Zweizig, Mary Jo Lynch, and Nancy A. VanHouse. *Planning and Role Setting for Public Libraries.* Chicago: American Library Association, 1987.

McConkey, Dale D. *Financial Management by Objectives.* Englewood Cliffs: Prentice-Hall, 1976.

Ordiorne, George S. *MBO II: A System for Managerial Leadership in the 80's.* Belmont, California: Fearon-Pitman, 1987.

Riggs, Donald. *Strategic Planning for Library Managers.* Phoenix: Oryx Press, 1984.

CHAPTER 6, CREATING BUDGETARY FORECASTS

Anderson, Lane K. and Donald K. Clancy. *Cost Accounting.* Homewood, Illinois: Irwin, 1990.

Barfield, Jesse T. *Cost Accounting: Traditions and Innovations.* St. Paul: West Publications, 1991.

Burgin, Robert. "Creative Budget Presentation: Using Statistics to Prove Your Point," *The Bottom Line* 1, 1 (1987): 13–17.

Dahlgren, Anders C. "Costing Library System Services," *The Bottom Line* 4, 3 (Fall 1990): 18–24.

Devlin, Barry. "Basic Budget Primer," *The Bottom Line* 2, 3 (1988): 20–24.

Koenig, Michael E. D. and Diedre Stam. "Budgeting and Financial Planning for Libraries," *Advances in Library Administration and Organization* 4 (1985): 77–110.

Murchio, Christine. "A Circulation System Cost Profile," *The Bottom Line* 1, 3 (1987): 20–24.

Palmour, Vernon E., Marcia C. Bellassai, and Nancy V. DeWath. *A Planning Process for Public Libraries.* Chicago: American Library Association, 1980.

Pasqalini, Bernard, ed. "Dollars and Sense: Implications of the New Online Technology for Managing the Library." Proceedings of the RASD Pre-conference, June 1986. Chicago: American Library Association, 1987.

Richmond, Elizabeth. "Cost-Finding: The Wisconsin Experience," *The Bottom Line* 2, 1 (1988): 23–28.

Richmond, Elizabeth. "Cost Finding: Method and Management," *The Bottom Line* 1, 4 (1987): 16–20.

Robinson, Barbara M. "Costing Question Handling and ILL/Photocopying," *The Bottom Line* 4, 2 (Summer 1990): 20–25.

Rosenberg, Philip. *Cost Finding for Public Libraries.* Chicago: American Library Association, 1985.

Sayre, Ed and Lee Thielen. "Cost Accounting: A Model for Small Libraries," *The Bottom Line* 3, 4 (1989): 15–19.

Sullivan, Timothy G. *How to Budget in a Service Organization.* Boston: American Management Associations Extension Institute, 1982.

Trumpeter, Margo and Richard Rounds. *Basic Budgeting Practices for Librarians.* Chicago: American Library Association, 1985.

Turock, Betty J. "Taking the Library Budget Out of the Twilight Zone," *Library Administration and Management* (Spring 1989): 65–67.

Vinson, Michael. "Cost-Finding: A Step-by-Step Guide," *The Bottom Line* 2, 3 (1989): 15–19.

Virgo, Julie. "Costing and Pricing Information Service," *Drexel Library Quarterly* (Summer 1985): 75–98.

CHAPTER 7, FUNDING STRATEGIES

Boulding, Kenneth. *A Preface to Grant Economics.* New York: Praeger, 1981.

Bradbury, Daniel J. "Seven Strategies for Effective Fund-Raising," *The Bottom Line* 2, 4 (1988): 11–14.

Clark, Charlene. "Going It Alone! Fundraising Without a Consultant," *The Bottom Line* 4, 4 (1990): 8–11.

Clay, Edwin S., III. "Fundraising by Strategic Design," *The Bottom Line* 1, 3 (1987): 25–27.

Cleary, Patricia M. "Investing with a Financial Safety Net," *The Bottom Line* 3, 3 (1989): 36.

Gertzog, Alice. "Gathering Grants—Financial Boon or Bust," *The Bottom Line*, Charter Issue (1986): 17–20.

Gilpatrick, Eleanor G. *Grants for Nonprofit Organizations: A Guide to Funding and Grant Writing.* New York: Praeger, 1989.

Goldberg, Susan. "Library Endowments: Building for Equity," *The Bottom Line* 4, 1 (Spring 1990): 22–23.

Hall, Richard B. "Winning a Bond Issue for a New Library," *The Bottom Line* 3, 2 (1989): 22–27.

McGovern, Gail. "Direct Mail Campaigns," *The Bottom Line* 1, 1 (1987): 35–37.

Miller, Robert C. "Endowment Funding in Academic Libraries," *The Bottom Line* 1, 1 (1987): 23–27.

Moran, Irene E. "Writing a Winning Grant Proposal," *The Bottom Line* 1, 2 (1987): 13–17.

Reidell, Mark. "The Joy of Staging Special Events," *The Bottom Line* 1, 4 (1987): 21–24.

Seltzer, Michael. *Securing Your Organization's Future: A Complete Guide to Fundraising Strategies.* New York: The Foundation Center, 1987.

Skloot, Edward, ed. *The Nonprofit Entrepreneur: Creating Ventures to Earn Income.* New York: Foundation Center, 1988.

CHAPTER 8, EVALUATING THE FINANCIAL PLAN

Bullin, Christine and John F. Rockart. "A Primer on Critical Success Factors." Center for Information Systems Research, Working Paper no. 69. Cambridge, Massachusetts: MIT, Sloan School of Management, 1981.

Carlzon, Jan. *Moments of Truth.* Cambridge, Massachusetts: Balinger, 1987.

Garvin, David A. *Managing Quality.* New York, Free Press, 1988.

Koontz, Harold, Cyril O'Donnell, and Heinz Weihrich. *Essentials of Management.* New York: McGraw-Hill, 1985.

Kosecoff, Jacqueline and Arlene Fink. *Evaluation Basics.* Beverly Hills: Sage Publications, 1982.

Lynch, Richard and Kevin F. Cross. *Measure Up!* Cambridge, Massachusetts: Basil Blackwell, 1991.

CHAPTER 9, WRAPPING IT UP

Brooks, Julie K. and Barry A. Stevens. *How to Write a Successful Business Plan*. New York: AMACOM Books, 1987.

Gumpert, David E. *How to Create a Successful Business Plan*. Boston: Inc. Publishing, 1990.

Siegel, S., Loren A. Schultz, Brian R. Ford, and David C. Carney. *The Ernst and Young Business Plan Guide*. New York: John Wiley, 1987.

Thurow, Lester. *The Zero Sum Society*. New York: Basic Books, 1980.

Thurow, Lester. *The Zero Sum Solution*. New York: Simon and Schuster, 1985.

Turock, Betty J. "Libraries and the Zero Sum Society," *The Bottom Line*, Charter Issue (1986): 3.

INDEX

Dr. Betty J. Turock is Chair of Library and Information Studies and Director of the MLS program at Rutgers University. She was the founding editor of *The Bottom Line: A Financial Magazine for Librarians*.

Andrea Pedolsky is Acquisitions Editor and Director of Editorial Development and Production at AMACOM Books, a division of the American Management Association.

Dr. Bill Katz is Professor at the School of Library and Information Science, State University of New York at Albany. He is the author of many distinguished works in library science.

Cover design: Apicella Design
Typography: Maryland Composition